The Reading Groups Book

ition

's 3

'& H

D0892447

The Reading Groups Book

2002–2003 Edition

Jenny Hartley

With a Survey Conducted in Association with
Sarah Turvey

Foreword by Margaret Forster

Illustrations by Ros Asquith

OXFORD
UNIVERSITY PRESS

OXFORD
UNIVERSITY PRESS

Great Clarendon Street, Oxford OX2 6DP

Oxford University Press is a department of the University of Oxford.
It furthers the University's objective of excellence in research, scholarship,
and education by publishing worldwide in

Oxford New York

Auckland Bangkok Buenos Aires Cape Town Chennai
Dar es Salaam Delhi Hong Kong Istanbul Karachi Kolkata
Kuala Lumpur Madrid Melbourne Mexico City Mumbai Nairobi
São Paulo Shanghai Singapore Taipei Tokyo Toronto
and an associated company in Berlin

Published in the United States
by Oxford University Press Inc., New York

© Jenny Hartley 2001, 2002

British Library Cataloguing in Publication Data

Data available

Library of Congress Cataloging in Publication Data

Data available

ISBN 0-19-925596-2

10 9 8 7 6 5 4 3 2 1

Typeset by Kolam Information Services Pvt. Ltd, Pondicherry, India
Printed in Great Britain
on acid-free paper by
T. J. International Ltd,
Padstow, Cornwall

for Nick

Foreword
By Margaret Forster

About two years ago, a letter arrived which intrigued me. It was from a woman who wrote saying that she was the secretary of a reading group and it was her job to provide some background to the writing of the book which the group intended to read that month, a memoir I'd written about my grandmother and mother, called *Hidden Lives*. She enclosed a list of questions which were easy enough to answer and I sent them back longing to ask questions of my own but not quite liking to, feeling a little embarrassed about my own intense curiosity. I tried instead to imagine what this reading group must be like. Was it composed entirely of women? Were they all women of a certain age? Bored housewives? How many of them were in the group? Did they meet in the afternoon or the evening? On the same day each month? Did they eat together, and if so before or after the discussion? And the discussion itself, what form did it take exactly? Was it merely a matter of exchanging views or was there a competitive edge to it? How were the books chosen? Was the prime purpose pleasure, or educational? Heavens, I wanted to know a lot.

From that time on, letters from other reading groups kept coming and I gradually formed my own theories about how and why they operated, helped also by the first-hand information I had from relatives and friends who belonged to them. I knew never to telephone my sister-in-law Annabel on the last Friday in every month because it was her reading-group meeting. Hers is a very relaxed, easy sort of group, only six people in it, and they simply swap details of books they have each read, saying why they liked them. They are unusual in all studying the same book only once a year. There seems nothing competitive about her group— it's all to do with sharing the pleasure of what has been read. My nephew Ross's reading group, on the other hand, is quite different. They are nearly all men in their twenties and they meet in a pub, arguing ferociously not just about what they've read (and giving books marks out of ten) but about the choosing of books to read (they all read the same book). Then there was my friend Margie, who seemed to worry quite a lot about how she would express her opinions, and another friend Liz who found one member of her group intimidating and dreaded it when it was this woman's turn to choose the book.

What, I wondered, is going on? Why, in the last decade of the twentieth century, this explosion of interest in forming groups with *reading* as the object? To me, reading has always been such a private thing, and I am such a solitude-loving person, that I find it baffling that others want to read together. I wished someone would come along and study this trend and explain its growth and examine its appeal. This is exactly what Jenny Hartley has done. I understand now how hard most people find it to snatch time to read and how, by belonging to a group, they make sure that they find it. I see how difficult it is for the majority of people to know what to read, and how, after they've read a book, they long to see what others have made of it. The social element is there, but this survey (though it is a lot more than just a survey) shows that it is secondary to a far greater desire to be stimulated by a spirited exchange of views. It is true that most groups do consist of women, and also true that the reading group is every bit as much a form of escape as belonging to any other sort of society, but it is an escape of a particularly satisfying sort in which the member is very actively engaged in a most enjoyable cultural exercise. As Jenny Hartley says, reading in a group is for so many people an anchor in their life which they quickly come to believe they cannot do without.

I am so glad to have had my curiosity satisfied by this book, a little bible for any reading group and quite an eye-opener for any writer. I learned more about my own books from hearing what certain reading groups have thought of them than I've ever done from any critic (and quite a shock some of these opinions were—what, moi, 'pretentious'?!).

Preface to the 2002-3 *Edition*

'Completely unlike anything else I do at home or work.'
'Going from strength to strength.'

Reading groups are, it seems, here to stay. When we started researching them at the end of 1998 we got a few blank looks: 'What *is* a reading group?' Now reading groups are hard to avoid. In the first years of the twenty-first century they have featured in Simpsons Cartoons and episodes of the Sopranos; and in the UK they have achieved their own TV show, Channel 4's surprise hit comedy, 'The Book Group'. So more people know what they are, and more people are joining one, sometimes more than one. Reading groups are undoubtedly a success story, and mark the arrival of a new and independent player on the literary scene: the active reader.

People have always read in groups of course, but the late 1990s saw an increase in their popularity and a corresponding flurry of media interest. We decided to find out more, and contacted 350 groups in the UK. No one knows just how many there are. Estimates run as high as 50,000 in Britain and 500,000 in America. This survey is the first of its kind, the tip of the tip of the iceberg.

We have tried to include the words of as many groups as possible. This was the best way to pass on our immediate sense of the distinct individuality of each group. And they are after all the experts. People in reading groups—some for over thirty years, some just beginning—are the ones who know best what works and what doesn't. They are going to have the hands-on experience as well as some of the best suggestions and ideas. And the variety is tremendous. Every group is different, has its own history, and finds its own way of doing things, engaged in what an American respondent called 'adventures in reading'.

The questionnaire we sent out in 1999 asks about the group: how long it has been going, how it started, how often and where it meets, how many there are in the group, and other information about gender, average age of group members, and so on. The second half of the questionnaire asks about what groups read, how they choose, and how they structure their discussions. We also ask for a list of books read recently, and what has gone particularly well or badly. We end by asking what people most enjoy about their groups, and if they would be prepared for one of us to sit in on a meeting so that we can get some idea of how groups talk. A shorter follow-up questionnaire was sent out at the end of 2001 to about 150 groups, to see how they were getting on and what they had read during the year.

This book describes the findings from our questionnaires and visits. The first chapter sets out what a reading group is, or rather the many things they can be, and some of their basic features. The second chapter looks at who belongs and how they started. Chapter 3, on how groups choose and what they read, gives a snapshot of reading choices at the end of the twentieth century. Chapter 4 focuses on how groups talk about their books and what makes for a good or bad session. As well as hearing from groups in the UK we have also heard from another hundred groups around the world, so the fifth chapter gives some idea of the global picture. Chapter 6 turns its attention to pleasure. Looking at what members say they most enjoy about their groups can give us a good sense of this thriving and expanding movement. Chapter 7 brings the story up to date. New for this edition, it looks at the findings of the 2001 questionnaire, and at the place and meaning of the reading group in the twenty-first century. The tables at the end set out the statistics. The appendix gives listings of useful books, guides, and websites, plus a selection from the many booklists which groups have compiled over the years. This new edition brings us up to date with suggestions from what groups were reading in 2001. 'What to read' is, some groups tell us, *the* question; these lists offer ways of answering it.

We made contact with reading groups through a range of sources. The telecommunications company Orange, whose Reading Groups promotion in 1997 sparked off huge interest, kindly mailed our questionnaire to groups registered with them, as did the *Mail on Sunday*'s *YOU* magazine. Through both we got a high level of response and our first glimpse of the vitality typical of reading groups. We also contacted groups via letters and announcements in the local and national press, and in journals and magazines: the *Times Literary Supplement*, *Woman*, the *People's Friend, Woman's Weekly*, and the *Good Book Guide*. We also appealed via Radio 4's *Open Book* programme and the Women's Institute journal *Home and Country*. Our aim was to find as many groups and as many different kinds of groups as possible. Groups also found us—through word of mouth, the powerful and distinctive engine of the reading group movement.

The positive response of groups to our requests for information is, I think, part of the whole phenomenon. They sent us long, detailed replies, considering each question carefully and giving us the benefit of their experiences and observations. Many sent us copies of reading lists, notes and minutes of meetings, annual newsletters, and reading diaries, sometimes going back over two decades. They opened their doors to us—'as long you bring wine/crisps/join in'—together with hospitable offers of overnight accommodation. The comments they made about filling in the questionnaire shed an unexpected light—both for them and for us—on their sense of themselves and what they value:

— *We enjoyed participating in the survey and thinking about our history.*

— *We enjoyed filling in the survey, it generated much animated discussion as we went through the list of books to see which ones we enjoyed the most and which we disliked the most and it also reminded us of books we had half forgotten.*

— *At our last book group meeting we put together the following answers to your questions, a process we found really enjoyable. A good chance to look back and talk together about what we do.*

The warmth and affection are almost tangible:

— *We all say it is pathetic how much we look forward to it— especially as we all have busy lives and demanding jobs.*

— *I regard these evenings as very special, removed from work and children and men, structured around a good book, which itself takes us beyond the narrow limits of our lives as well as allowing us to explore our inner feelings. It is an inspired combination.*

— *Everybody adores it. We all like each other very much.*

Metropolitan journalists may sneer at 'the virtues of middle-class England's new favourite night out';[1] but when someone describes her group as 'the best thing that's happened to me for ages', and she is not alone, it seems to be worth taking a closer look at what some of these groups do and say.

Acknowledgements

The questionnaires were designed, distributed, and collected by Sarah Turvey and myself. Apart from the writing up the project has been a joint one, and Sarah's expertise, wisdom, and involvement have been vital. We would both like to thank the many people without whom we could not have completed the survey. Their interest, knowledge, and enthusiasm for the project have helped immeasurably.

We are particularly indebted to Orange, and to the *Mail on Sunday*'s *YOU* magazine, for sending our questionnaires to groups registered with them. This gave our research a huge boost, as did the interest and active support of Liz Attenborough, director of the National Year of Reading. We would also like to thank all the colleagues, friends, and reading group contacts who helped by offering first-hand knowledge and in collecting information from an array of sources we could not possibly have mustered by ourselves. Our thanks go especially to Ian Britain and Barbara Anderson in Australia, Margaret Bertulli in Canada, Phyllis Lassner and Janet Stern in Illinois, Jessica Munns in Denver, Margo Miller in Boston, Mass., Judy Breen in San Francisco, Elizabeth Long in Houston, Janet Murphy and her global network, Sue Godfree in France, Tom Palmer in Bradford, Michael Booker in Bristol, and the Decagon group, Liz Kirby, Professor Ann Thompson, Honor Wilson-Fletcher, Elaine Moss, Charles

Stern, Jean Seaton, Jane Pimlott, and Judy Routledge in London. We would also like to thank Felicity Lander, Jan Daws, Jane Pringle, Oriane Haldane, and Cathy Wells-Cole at the University of Surrey Roehampton for their involvement, Kate Jones and Louisa Symington at Penguin for sharing reading group data, and Genevieve Clarke at the National Reading Campaign for keeping us in touch with the latest initiatives. We are grateful to conference organizers at Napier University, Edinburgh and the University of Surrey Roehampton for inviting us to give papers on this work at an early stage. We received welcome funding from the Research Department of the University of Surrey Roehampton, and timely computer help from Ned Hartley. Nick Hartley's statistical expertise was indispensable, we are grateful to him for long hours of labour.

A survey such as this relies on the goodwill of those taking part, and we are indebted to all the groups who have contributed so generously. We would like to express our appreciation for all you have done for us—giving your time, support, and inside knowledge, and making the whole project such a pleasure. To all of you, our heartfelt thanks.

J.H.

Contents

One

What is a Reading Group?

'The longest relationship I've ever been in.'

Reading in groups has been around for as long as there has been reading. A history of it would fill a book, probably a shelf. The Romans did it, emigrants on board ship to Australia did it, Schubert and his friends meeting to read and discuss the poems of Heine were doing it. In the centuries before printing and cheap books, when books or manuscripts had to be shared and read aloud, there must have been some discussion or commentary, however brief. In fifteenth-century France a group of women who gathered to spin during the long winter evenings took turns to read aloud to each other. They chose from the recent spate of books written 'against the honour of the female sex', and thoroughly enjoyed accompanying the readings with a rich barrage of commentary (their male chronicler finds such 'laxity' tiresome).[1] We may think of reading as something solitary and private—'the lone voyage', it's sometimes called—but the impulse to share can be powerful. Susan Sibbald, who lived in the eighteenth century when books were still very expensive, was driven to copying out whole volumes in long-hand so that she could 'share her favourite reading with a friend'.[2] In our own times, a Waterstone's survey finds that 'nine out of ten adults enjoy talking about reading to friends'.[3] And if reading in groups has a long past, it is also an experience with deep roots in our own personal histories. Our earliest encounters with books were most probably as children with a parent and perhaps a sibling, a small group characterized by intimacy and pleasure.

While reading groups are an important part of many people's lives—'the highlight of my week' according to a member of a rural group—to others they have been more or less invisible. A reading group can be many things, since it's any group which wants to call itself one. The usual minimal definition would be a group of people who meet on a regular basis to discuss books. People who responded to our survey of groups in the UK and filled in a questionnaire about their reading group included 'the head of a family', and two friends who meet in each other's kitchens and make a third with a sister through her letters from America. At the other end of the scale are the cybergroups who roam the web, never meeting face to face. This chapter maps some of the many different groups that are currently flourishing: where they happen, how big they are, and how long they've been going. We start with the global group.

Internet reading groups are legion, transient, and diverse, forming excited and impermanent communities of talk. They may spring from special-interest groups like the Brit/Aussies Mystery Reading Group or fans swapping obscure knowledge of a cult author such as Neil Gaiman. Sometimes a solitary reader wants to share his or her latest enthusiasm: 'I've just blown my mind with *Catch 22*' reports Keith from Wolverhampton, while Amazon encourages everyone to join in the reviewing process. Any account of the net's assets runs the risk of obsolescence, but the resources it offers are unique, and an hour or so's browsing can be highly entertaining. Quite a few groups in our survey say they use the net (see Chapter 4); a good introduction for UK first-timers is Bradford Library's *Book Lover's Guide to the Internet*.

The internet can best be seen in two ways: as an aid for reading groups, and as a reading group in itself (see Appendix: Websites for listings). Resources, often provided by publishers and large bookshops, range from discounts to author interviews and extracts from new titles. Or you can go fishing on your own to find out more about your books and authors: with a bit of practice you can usually land a juicy morsel or two. You can also get your books chosen for you by Book Forager. Choose what sort of book you want along a series of sliding scales (for example 'short/long', 'gentle/violent', 'no sex/sex', 'optimistic/bleak') and Forager comes up with suggestions. Groups might enjoy a Forager book occasionally for a lucky-dip night. I asked for something 'funny', 'frightening', and 'unpredictable' and Forager suggested Geoff Nicholson's *Footsucker*, along with the reader comment: 'A disturbing comic novel about a foot and shoe fetishist. Lots of graphic deviant sex and a plot which includes murder. Unpleasantly compulsive.'[4]

What about the net as a reading-group provider and host? Although UK readers are catching on to the net as a resource, Americans are ahead in exploiting its potential for collective reading. Some groups are open to all who want to join in; others may be face-to-face groups which aren't open but like to broadcast their events. Online reading groups running in real time (rather than bulletin boards where you post your comments) may be the next big thing, with the US blazing an enthusiastic trail. In the UK Bradford Libraries, pioneers in the field, launched a site in spring 1999 for ten virtual reading groups, attracting readers from all over the world.[5] Altogether, although the internet may seem the opposite of what reading groups value (the face to face, the local), it can be welcomed with open arms as a wonderful resource: not a substitute but a supplement, and a good second best for the housebound or the isolated.

Reading groups famously went mass media in 1996 in America with Oprah's Book Club, one of the most staggering phenomena in the history of collective reading. The talk-show host Oprah Winfrey announced that she wanted to 'get the country reading', and she seems to have done just that. Each month she would choose a book, and a month later half a show would be devoted to discussing it.

The show receives as many as 10,000 letters each month from people eager to participate. By the time the segment appears, 500,000 viewers have read at least part of the book. Nearly as many buy the book in the weeks that follow. This approach has made Winfrey the most successful pitch person in the history of publishing. Since its debut in 1996, Oprah's Book Club has been responsible for 28 consecutive bestsellers. It has sold more than 20m books and made many of its authors millionaires. It has earned publishers roughly $175m...a vast experiment in linked literary imagination and social engineering. Toni Morrison calls it 'a revolution', because Winfrey's rapport with the camera cuts across class and race.[5]

The effect on the nation's reading habits was palpable: Toni Morrison's *Song of Solomon* sold as many copies in six weeks as in the previous nine years. A 46-year-old woman confessed that until her conversion to reading through Oprah she had not read more than five books in her entire life. But by April 2002 the craze seemed to have abated a little. Sales of endorsed books had dropped from an extra million to 600,000; and Winfrey announced that she would be curtailing her book club segments because 'it had become too difficult to find personally compelling offerings every month.'[6]

The UK's answer to Oprah is the broadcaster James Naughtie, host of Radio 4 Bookclub. The programme, with its audience of half a million and growing, was launched by producer Olivia Seligman in 1998; she saw it as 'a natural radio thing'. The author usually attends, fielding questions, comments, and sometimes criticism from an audience of twenty-five, drawn from reading groups around the country. In Naughtie's words, it's 'a readers' conversation, not a critics' conversation', and there is an unexpected democracy about the studio as the author becomes one of the discussion group. 'I couldn't disagree more', said Ian McEwan at one point during the discussion of *Enduring Love* that I sat in on; but it was said without rancour or pulling rank or closing down the argument. Naughtie and Seligman both relish such moments, which give the programme its bite. By listening to this programme together, some of the groups in our survey turn the macro-group of listeners into their own micro-group of active readers.

Groups which meet face to face rather than online or through other media are of course the bulk of the reading-group movement. Sometimes they owe their birth to a parent organization such as a public library, the University of the Third Age, or the Women's Institute. The idea got a big boost in the UK in 1997, with the promotion by the Orange tele-communications company of its Reading Group pack. Five thousand of these packs were eagerly snapped up, and they are still sought after. In 1998 the *Mail on Sunday*'s *YOU* magazine launched its monthly reading group, selecting a book to offer at discount, together with an interview with the author and an 'expert analysis of the book, which you can use as the basis for discussion, whether you're in an established reading group or would simply like to use us as your reading partner'. By the end of 2001, 150,000 readers had taken advantage of the scheme, including groups who like having their books picked for them by a third party—'this way no one has to take the blame'. By the late 1990s the reading group had arrived on the market map, with a supermarket offering groups discounts on its website, and *Good Housekeeping* magazine teaming up with the Ottakar's bookshop chain to offer discounts, reading guides, and tips on how to get started.

Bookshops have a good history of providing readers with congenial social spaces. Mrs Arlbery, the witty older woman in Fanny Burney's 1796 novel *Camilla*, passes many pleasant hours at the Tunbridge bookseller's, where she has her own special seat.

Here, that lady was soon joined by Lord O'Lerney and General Kinsale, who were warm admirers of her vivacity and observation. Mr Dennel took up the *Daily Advertiser*; his daughter stationed herself at the door to see the walkers upon the Pantiles; Sir Theophilus Jarard, under colour of looking at a popular pamphlet, was indulging in a nap in a corner; Lord Newford, noticing nothing, except his own figure as he past a mirrour, was shuffling loud about the floor, which was not much embellished by the scraping of his boots; and Sir Sedley Clarendel, lounging upon a chair in the middle of the shop, sat eating *bon bons*.[7]

Groups in today's bookshops do more reading; they may comprise a shifting population dropping in, attracted by a particular book or topic, or they may be longer-lasting. Safe and familiar yet not too intimate—nobody's personal territory—the bookshop is a good place for special-interest groups. Gay groups, poetry groups, science fiction and crime fiction groups can all be found in bookshops. A gay group has been running on the third Tuesday of the month in the Earls Court Waterstone's since 1996: an American customer brought the idea and enthused staff to set one up. Titles are suggested by members, who get a 20 per cent discount off group books. These will have a gay content or aspect, but 'often only broadly—we've done Iris Murdoch's *The Bell*, for instance'. Borders opened its Oxford Street shop in London in 1998 with a well-publicized set of groups run by keen staff members. Mesteret, the organizer of the Blackberry group, chose to focus on work by black British writers because she felt that the British experience was 'getting a bit lost' in the general profile of black writing. A lively session on Jackie Kay's *Trumpet* brought together a mix of women, black and white; those of us who did not have copies of the book (only available at that time in hardback) were loaned bookshop copies. One woman was a knowledgeable fan of Kay's poetry; another worked in a barber's and supplied useful information about transvestism and shaving. In a new departure, the *Guardian* newspaper used groups based at Borders bookshops in Glasgow, London, Brighton, and Leeds to help choose the winner of the 1999 *Guardian* First Book Award.

Initiatives such as these show that publishers and book-sellers in the UK are waking up to the potential of the reading-group market, but quite slowly. Just over half of the 268 booksellers contacted for a survey conducted in February 2000 by Book Marketing Ltd. said they had some involvement with reading groups, and for the most part this was by offering a discount—but only one in three of the bookshops in the survey do this. And only 10 per cent of those involved with reading groups 'allow the use of store as venue'. Even fewer distribute guides, advertise for new members, or keep a register of local groups. Some of the booksellers come across in this survey as cool to the point of indifference; others are starting to move towards a more positive relationship. The survey also got returns from fourteen publishers, six of whom had some involvement with reading groups, mainly through producing guides. Lack of time and resources, as well as 'no demand from reading groups' were the reasons given for non-involvement;[8] though one new British publishing house has clearly got the message. Persephone Books, founded by the critic and biographer Nicola Beauman in 1999, is set not only to appeal to many reading groups, but also to create one for the reader at home, with a quarterly newsletter and carefully selected list.[9]

Public libraries are also mobilizing on the reading-group front, in line with the current emphasis on reader development. The appointment of Reader Development Officers and other initiatives, some of them born during the National Year of Reading (1998–9), have been popular.[10] Groups pay tribute to the help and support they have had:

— *With some good publicity and excellent co-operation from Letchworth Library our group has gone from strength to strength.*

A library group in Wexford has men and women ranging from the late twenties to the mid-sixties:

— *As well as the titles under discussion, most members head out the door at midnight with an armful of books. One of the most enjoyable elements of the evening is the final raid of the library shelves with members sharing recommendations.*

Public libraries facilitate groups by ordering sets of books, providing venues, and perhaps a member of staff to co-ordinate (some have been on courses on how to set up a group). The goal of Essex Libraries is to have at least one reading group per library (they have seventy-four branches), and they now have a hundred active groups 'in all shapes and sizes'. These groups mainly borrow books, with existing stock big enough to cope as groups choose for themselves, 'with a bit of guidance to steer them away from costly new hardbacks'. Readers in residence can help groups choose, publish book profiles, and organize readers into book chains. Bradford Libraries also run Readers, an annual day of talks and author events for reading groups.[11] Leaders of library groups, usually members of library staff, find the experience worthwhile:

— *I wanted to encourage readers to share their experiences of books with each other and extend the range of material they try.*

— *I enjoy getting to know people much better than I am able to when I meet them as borrowers at the enquiry desk of the library.*

— *I get the pleasure of introducing readers to new authors.*

— *Immense pleasure when a book I've recommended finds favour with the group.*

Libraries also have an important part to play in book supply. Most of the groups in our survey buy their books, and usually have a paperback-only rule—canny groups scour remainder stores. But quite a lot borrow, occasionally from a mobile library, more often with help from the local library:

— *Must thank Sutton Coldfield Library staff who are brilliant. I now hand in a list of what we want to read each month at the beginning of the year and they sort it all out—all I have to do is collect and return books.*

— *We mainly borrow from our very co-operative village library who obtain books from all over the county.*

— *I have linked up with the library and obtained a ticket to borrow books which have been read by other groups and which they therefore have multiple copies of.*

Groups meeting in libraries account for 6 per cent of the groups in our survey; a further 14 per cent meet in other public spaces, such as pubs, bars, cafés, pizza restaurants, and health and fitness centres, or 'a quiet corner of the Royal Festival Hall' (Table 4). Younger groups are more likely to meet in such places:

— *We wanted a neutral ground away from distractions.*

Groups also meet in mental hospitals and prisons, in works canteens, staff-rooms, residential homes for the elderly, and day centres for the blind. The National Library for the Blind runs an 'in-house' group for its members, both sighted and non-sighted. Because of problems with availability of books for the visually impaired, they often pick themes rather than particular books, or a genre such as short stories. These went down well:

— *Everyone said they didn't like/read them, and then talked enthusiastically about the three examples.*

A Harley Street dentist's waiting room is also a venue, as is the zoo, this last for the group specializing in animal stories.

Quite a few of the groups in our survey have grown out of the workplace, a tradition with a long history:

— *In a [British] milltown in the late 1840s, a group of girl operatives met at five o'clock in the morning to read Shakespeare together for an hour before going to work.*[12]

These days it's probably after work, and not Shakespeare.

— *It's a good way to get to know work people better.*

— *We enjoy the socialization outside the workplace.*

The caring professions, who know the value of talk, have generated some thriving work-based groups. In the US there are groups whose members all work with emotionally disturbed children or in medical centres; in the UK a group who all work in adoption agencies. According to this group:

— *It is an advantage all working in the same field. We all enjoyed Jackie Kay's* Trumpet *because it was about adoption, which is the area we all work in. Obviously adoption is a device which many writers use. It also has important issues about loss which relate to our work.*

The group at the Institute of Cancer Research have a big mailing list of forty-five and about twenty usually come. The institute subsidizes some of the books, which are then donated to the Royal Marsden Hospital. Damian Counsell, an unpaid organizer, finds it very rewarding and points out that 'workplace dos tend to be of the office party variety, and we've had people along who wouldn't come to social events normally; it's a good excuse for meeting up outside work'. Other workplace groups take advantage of *YOU* discounts and enjoy canteen discussions of the monthly choice.

Orange's 1999 Orange Talks Books at Work was designed to promote reading groups in the workplace; Orange itself has twenty-two in-house reading groups. The company provides a room, lunch, and some free books and discounts to get groups up and running. Members come together from across the company—directors as well as customer services staff. Groups choose their own books, swapping opinions and reading suggestions throughout the company on an internal internet page. The six groups at Marks and Spencer's head office also contain a mix from different areas of the business, and all run independently. The company provides encouragement and a room for groups to meet at lunchtime. It is well known in Britain that times have not been easy for this large company, and Julia Havis, the company's Arts and Science Forum manager, and initial enthusiast for groups in the company, has noticed that these groups are particularly valuable in bringing people closer together: 'It makes you appreciate what other people are going through.'

British companies may provide rooms, lunches, and subsidized books; they are supportive, but in a hands-off way. Work-based groups in the US have been more openly business-focused, as the group writing in Ellen Slezak's *Book Group Book* explains:

On May 19 1993, the company held its first book club luncheon [at a local hotel]. It was organized in an effort to capture some of the great business ideas already discovered and published in books, and so far it is working. Books are chosen through suggestions from the group. Each month a new book with a business-related topic is introduced to the company and made available to anyone who wants to participate.

Everyone in the company is invited to the meeting—from the newest entry-level clerks on up through the ranks of the senior officers. The group is truly a collage of the company—secretaries, accountants, lawyers, and marketers. Our president hosts the luncheon for the month's participants, where they discuss the morsels of truth and knowledge found in the books, and then talk about how they can apply them to AAL Capital Management Corporation.[13]

While a group at Marks and Spencer have been reading Michael Frayn's Booker nominee, *Headlong* ('absolutely great'), the American list includes Bill Fromm's *The 10 Commandments of Business* and William C. Byham's *ZAPP! The Lightning of Empowerment*. But although British management styles might make a less literal connection between book and workplace, the faith in the bonus for the company is none the less. The interpersonal skills, flexibility, and openness to new ideas, the teamwork, and the ability to communicate so valued in today's employees are exactly those qualities which the reading group can be so good at cultivating. It can also benefit cross-cultural sensitivity and what have been referred to as 'complexity skills'—the ability to manage 'ambiguous situations where many events and trends are interlinked'.[14]

The vast majority of reading groups in our survey are neighbourhood groups: neighbours and friends who live within reasonable distance of each other. Indeed for some groups geographical proximity is a defining or significant factor.

— *I set up the group with friends and invited other friends—stipulation of being local.*

— *We all live in same or adjoining roads.*

— *Most live in the same village and we can normally walk to the meetings.*

— *Started by a group of neighbours who wanted a reason to socialize.*

Neighbourhood is one of the motives which prompts people to start, join, and stay in a group. The group is itself a micro-neighbourhood, and usually sets its timetable to behave as one with neighbourhood talk (gossip). It behaves as a neighbourhood too in its predilection for word of mouth as its favoured means of communication. Word of mouth is, as we found early in our research, the crucial motor in reading-group dynamics and a big factor in their popularity. These two features—neighbourhood and word of mouth—are what reading groups are really all about: face-to-face communication. Running against the tides of all-encompassing mass media, long-distance link-ups, and global horizons, reading groups partly owe their success to their commitment to the smaller circle of known faces, to the idea of loyalty to the small scale and direct contact. A buffer and bulwark against 'out there', reading groups are the grass roots communicating with the global.

The commitment to the local manifests itself in various ways. Groups often like to form firm relationships with a local bookshop:

— *We've arranged a 10 per cent discount with our local independent bookshop. We've tried to steer clear of the big bookselling chains as we like to do our bit to keep our local bookshop in business.*

— *The local bookseller brings a selection to the meeting twice a year and gives a brief talk on the books.*

They also involve themselves in local issues or charitable causes such as sponsorship.

— *One meeting a year to raise funds for children by organizing a meal using period recipes.*

Given the importance of neighbourhood to reading groups, it's not surprising to find that by far the majority of groups, 80 per cent, meet in people's homes (Table 4).[15] This domestic location contributes significantly to the whole experience. Atmosphere is crucial to how groups talk, and what they clearly value is the safe space in which people can, usually literally, feel 'at home'. Trust is vital to a group, as is its social well-being, and quite early in their lives groups will often develop distinctive patterns and rituals to bond them together. Sometimes it will be a striking name—the Lang Whang Readers,[16] La Scala, Books We Always Meant To Read, the M25 Group, the Highbury Highbrows ('don't take the name too seriously!'), STILRAB (Stuff The Internet Let's Read A Book)—and sometimes even quite informal groups will have well-understood rules, as we'll see later.

Food and drink, it's not surprising to find, have an important part to play, in rituals which can get quite elaborate. Practically every group in our survey serves food and drink of some kind, if only tea and biscuits. Indeed some groups are keen that it should only be tea and biscuits, and forbid competitive catering:

— *When the cooking took over from the reading, the cooking had to stop.*

— *A while ago we argued a lot over the food/drink formula and downgraded from a meal bought and shared by everyone, to soup provided by the host. This works well, it's nice and simple.*

— *Nothing but bought biscuits to be served, to prevent people feeling obliged to outdo each other in hospitality and provide curry for Indian books etc.*

Books plus restaurant can be the solution:

— *We're now going to combine the reading group with a shared enjoyment for eating out.*

Another group admitted its true agenda and came out as a dining group; for others the cake *must* be home-baked. Some alcohol, usually wine, is a necessary adjunct, and men's groups in particular can be quite rule-bound about their drink:

— *The bottle of whisky is opened at ten o'clock and must be finished by the end of the evening.*

Port, Madeira, and perfectly cut sandwiches (no shop-bought substitutes will do) are stipulated for other all-male groups— who also have a weakness for jam tarts. The meal can be central to the evening, whether or not it's in a restaurant.

Members may take it in turns to cook and serve lunches, suppers, or three-course meals. The host of one men's group takes the day off to prepare, and the next to recover. A popular variant is to match book of the night with dish of the day, though this may work better on the page than the plate—the suggestion of left-overs to go with *The Remains of the Day* was wisely abandoned. But the group whose hostess made the recipes in Norah Ephron's *Heartburn* had a great evening. Eating can of course be the driving force: the name of the New Jersey group, Mostly We Eat, gives their game away. Their food and book combinations, helpfully posted on the net, can be intriguing: exactly what were the 'subversive and oppressive foods' served with Bohumil Hrabal's *Too Loud a Solitude*, and were they edible?[17] Other groups co-ordinate text with location for their weekends away: a windmill for *Don Quixote*, Lyme Regis for *Persuasion*.

Members of a reading group will usually all read the same book for their meeting, so that they can discuss it together; but there are some groups who operate differently. They may read up to three books for each session, or each pick different books by the same author (for example Terry Pratchett), or different books on an agreed theme—this makes borrowing easier. An eighteen-year-old rural group was started by a woman who belonged to a book club in South Africa:

— *Each lady has a turn to talk about the books she has read during the month. Every three months we all read the same book and discuss it.*

In south-west London in the inter-war years members of a magazine group paid an annual subscription of about 12s. (60p) to put them on the circulation list of a range of quality weeklies and monthlies such as *Strand Magazine*, *Cornhill*, *Chambers' Journal*, *Punch*, the *Illustrated London News*, *Tatler*, and *Country Life*—a huge variety of reading material coming into the house. Membership passed down through families; our informant remembered being recruited by her mother.

Readers occasionally pass single copies of books round the circle. This is what one of the longest-running groups in our survey, the Bristol Friendly Reading Society, does. Twenty-four men meet on the third Monday of the month, each man taking his turn to host the group in his house, much as the custom was started in October 1799. In those days it was a mug of ale and a churchwarden pipe for each Friend; now it's coffee, biscuits, and port. The secretary brings a selection of new books and Friends make their choice; the books circulate round the Friends and are auctioned at a twice-yearly sale. The original rule book set an annual subscription of one guinea, so today's rate of £25 has kept well below inflation. The views and activities of the poet Coleridge and his publisher Joseph Cottle may have influenced the society, and during that auspicious October of 1799 Coleridge was indeed in Bristol, where he was introduced to laughing gas by Humphry Davy. This was a time when, according to Coleridge's biographer Richard Holmes, 'Every city had its Dissenting society or reading group...regard[ing] themselves, with some justice, as the progressive intellectual elite of the nation'.[18] The Bristol Friendly Reading Society, which was founded by the members of two Dissenting chapels, has always been a neighbourhood group. In the past Friends lived within walking distance of each other, which helped the circulation of books each Monday (grumbles are minuted from one member in the 1880s who had a fifteen-minute walk). Efforts are made, according to Michael Booker, the current secretary, who has been a Friend for thirty-six years (and to whom I am happily indebted for generous hospitality and a comprehensive knowledge of the society), to 'keep a balance between those living in the city and those in the country, between the various professions and to some extent between age groups'. Thus in the present membership the professions (legal, medical, and academic) are well represented, as are the Church, business, and the media. Farmers, bishops, and television executives meet to discuss books in a tradition which goes back 200 years. The best way to understand the way the Bristol Friendly Reading Society works is to see it as a library in miniature, with up to a hundred books in circulation at a time. It puts handsome bookplates in its books, clothes them in practical plastic jackets, and pastes a label in the front, so that Friends may write their names and comments if they wish. Records, which date back to the 1880s, provide a fascinating history of reading habits and responses. And, extraordinarily, Bristol still has at least three other reading societies which date back to the early nineteenth century. The Social Book Club was reconstituted in 1833 from a previous book club, 'the monthly meetings of which', according to a founder-member of the new group, 'had lapsed into unduly late hours spent over cards and wine'.

Most groups, however, meet to discuss the book that everyone has read for the occasion, a different book each time—though there are of course variations, individuality being the hallmark of the reading-group movement. Some groups are, for instance, stuck on one book, as we will see in Chapter 3. Since most of the groups we have heard from are neighbourhood groups and their main stronghold the home, the 'front-room factor' determines the size of the group. Just over half the groups in our survey (57 per cent) have between six and ten members (Table 2). Just over a quarter (27 per cent) have between eleven and fifteen members; there seem to be more larger groups in the country, more of the very small groups (under five members) in urban areas. Respondents have definite views on the 'right' size for their group:

— *We now number eight, and after discussion we've decided we want to keep it that way—we like the closeness and if it's too big we can't all fit in the room. I've had complete strangers ring up to ask if they can join and have been able to redirect them to a few other local groups I know of.*

— *We discussed the admission of a ninth person some time ago, but came down against it on the grounds of group dynamics and because eight seemed the ideal number.*

— *We know we are an unusually large group (twelve) which has some disadvantages, but any attempt to divide us into two groups (e.g. one specializing in the contemporary novel) has been fiercely resisted. We like the mix (of age and background) and the attendance level is gratifying.*

— *At fourteen we feel we are full.*

A twenty-three-year-old group of thirteen decided that 'it would become too unwieldy if we had more people'—their most recent member joined twelve years ago. A group may take a few years to find its 'ideal number'; it will then stick at its four or fourteen, and new blood will not always be a bonus, as a member of a seven-year-old group comments:

— *One request to join was agreed but did not work. Other requests turned down! Main reason—we now have a 'literary history' of books read and discussed, as well as a social history—marriages/births/separation, etc.*

A group of five always gets 100 per cent attendance: it seems that the smaller the number the better the attendance rate. Some groups circulate their reading lists to a wider circle of non-attending but interested readers.

Most groups meet monthly (Table 5). The most frequent exceptions are to meet every six or eight weeks, or in term-time only, for those with school-age children. Many groups have summer breaks, or a special 'non-book' get-together at Christmas when they may be too busy to read. A few groups meet weekly or fortnightly, and work-based ones on an ad hoc basis. One group meets three or four times a year and covers three books a time: each book is introduced by someone who has done a written review.

Reading groups may seem to be a new thing, suddenly visible in the UK.[19] Our figures collected in 1999–2000 (Table 1) indicate that while 38 per cent of the groups are relatively young, a surprising 21 per cent have been going for over ten years, and a 'group of mothers wishing to discuss something other than potty-training' is still going strong twenty-eight years later. Nearly a quarter of the rural groups are over ten years old, and larger groups seem to have staying power: 20 per cent have been going for more than ten years

(Table 2). What we seem to be seeing now is a resurgence. Groups spring into life as a Mexican wave surges through a neighbourhood. The survey reveals a series of hot spots of new group activity—round St Albans in Hertfordshire for instance, paralleling what seems to have happened in Bristol two centuries ago.

A reading group isn't just about reading; it's about reading in a context, a context which is fostered by the group, and which in turn affects the whole experience of reading. In a way group behaviour can be a bit like a well-functioning family. They like, for example, to celebrate special occasions, mark anniversaries, and go on outings together. Groups in our survey mention going to the theatre and literary festivals together; they organize Christmas meetings in pubs, visits to places with literary connections, and annual weekends away. Or they may join for a meeting with one or two other reading groups in the neighbourhood. One group saves its air-miles to get them to the south of France in December; another group got its members away to Norfolk to celebrate its thirtieth birthday. Given that some of these groups have lasted longer than many marriages, their anniversaries certainly seem worth celebrating.

Reading groups, then, are not any one thing, but as various and diverse as their members. Clearly they share certain things in common. 'The books, the people' is in a nutshell the most frequent answer to our question 'What do you most enjoy about your reading group?' But even here some would diverge. One respondent told us we should have asked what made members stay in a group. We thought this unnecessary, being to do with pleasure—after all, no one forces you to go. No, she said, she didn't enjoy the discussions or the people very much (everyone disagreed with her); she stayed because she liked having her reading chosen for her, books she would never have chosen for herself. Reading groups may all look alike from a distance, but each group is different and relishes that difference, often comparing itself favourably with other groups (reading groups always know other groups). In the following chapters we look at some of the different groups in our survey: who is in them and what they read.

Two

Who Belongs to Reading Groups?

'All human life is here.'

What does our survey tell us about the people who belong to reading groups? The most obvious and unsurprising thing is that most of them are women. All-female groups account for 69 per cent of the groups; 4 per cent are all-male (Table 7). If we exclude the groups contacted via Orange (the association with the Orange Prize might lead to a female bias), the figure for all-female groups is still high, at 66 per cent, with all-male groups at 6 per cent. As we have seen, some of the oldest groups, with the more formal traditions, are all-male. When the youngest member of one such group proposed inviting women he was reminded, 'women can start their own groups'; and of course women have, so much so that reading groups now tend to be seen, usually dismissively, as 'a women's thing'. But many of the book clubs which sprang up throughout the UK in the eighteenth century were almost exclusively male. The oldest group still going which we have come across started with seventeen men in Dalton-in-Furness in Cumbria in 1764: seventeen men and seventeen rules, and a register which is still kept. The Dalton Book Club, like the Bristol Friendly Reading Society, is a circulating book club, and members make their choices according to long-established procedures. There is a strong element of social ritual in their monthly meetings, which invariably start with members sitting 'around the edge of their room' (always licensed premises):

— *in order of seniority of membership, beginning to the left of the chairman . . . Only after making their choices, and clearly calling out the numbers of their selected books for the secretary to record, do the participants approach the table and order two rounds (no more) of beer. . . . There is still an unwritten rule that each member shall fill his own glass, and none other, and each member is solemnly warned by the president: 'Fill what you will, but drink what you fill'.*

More rules about drinking: 'At one time there was a rule that when a member becomes the Senior—now the president—he pays a bottle of rum, and when he has been a member for fifty years he pays a bottle of brandy. Eight of our past members have had this distinction.'[1]

Although these men-only reading groups are now rare, there are more mixed groups in the survey than we expected, and the figure of 27 per cent seems fairly constant whatever the age of the group. The tradition is not new. By the early nineteenth century women's names are starting to appear on membership lists. The 'List of Members belonging to the

Reading Society held at Mr Tibnam's, Bookseller, Wyle Cop, Shrewsbury', which I have in my possession, seems to date from the first half of the nineteenth century; it consists of fourteen women and three men (one Reverend, one MP, two women with titles, and six married and six unmarried women). Also in the West Country, 'gentlemen's and ladies' book clubs' are mentioned in Richard Polwhele's 1806 *History of Cornwall*. Polwhele particularly admires the Roseland club, 'composed of ladies and gentlemen indiscriminately...a most respectable society [among whom] none but publications of the first order are circulated. The club's anniversary dinner is an occasion of elegance and refined enjoyment, contrasting with the too frequent scenes of uproar, profaneness, and vulgarity.'[2] And at the other end of England William Wordsworth was enjoying himself at the Kendal Book Club annual Venison Feast and Book Club Ball.[3]

If we look at the age of members in our survey, four of the five groups of under thirties are mixed—a tiny sample but possibly an interesting trend. Nearly a third of the groups of widely varied age are mixed, and the older the members the more likely the group is to be mixed. Presumably this has to do with men retiring, though most of the women in the survey are in paid work. Some mixed groups consist partly of couples (more so in the US than the UK), but this tends not to be something couples do together. In mixed groups women often predominate, and a character called 'our token male' appears on quite a few surveys, a welcome but sometimes fleeting figure:

— *Alas men are hard to come by but we really like to have them— their comments are always different.*

— *We welcome both sexes and find generally that the men always see the book in a different light to the women.*

The dearth of men is often commented on:

— *Can't find any men who read.*

— *Our husbands don't read very much.*

— *Not only are our husbands slower readers generally but seem shy of joining in a discussion of what they have read.*

— *Tried a mixed group but it didn't work.*

— *Men have come but don't last.*

— *All female by design.*

— *All female—we want to keep it like that.*

— *We are wary of introducing males at this stage.*

All-female groups reflect on the reasons for as well as the benefits of segregation:

— *Women take more pleasure in verbalizing their feelings and re-actions.*

— *Men don't seem to enjoy the 'process' of discussion as much—they have a firm opinion on something and that is that.*

— *We enjoy being independent from men with meaningful, intelligent conversations.*

— *At one time we thought about having men in the group. Originally (eighteen years ago) it was a group formed of women friends, and our husbands became interested and envious of the pleasure we had from our book reading and discussion and wanted to join us, but we felt that the balance of the group would be upset and possibly the men would dominate or take over the group and the women would slide into the background and make the tea, as has happened so often in the past with mixed groups. We decided not to make the change and suggested that they form their own group.*

— *In a way the whole point is that we're all women . . . with a man present the whole tone would be entirely different. Not that we'd defer to male authority—not at all—but our discussions are somehow humane and intuitive and exploratory rather than cerebral.*

Gender is related to genesis. Many of the all-female groups started as mothers with young children:

— *I started the group to use my brain and talk about something other than babies.*

— *It started off as time away from children, and to talk about something stimulating.*

— *After I'd had my baby and left work, I decided I must do something to prevent brain death and contacted a few friends.*

— *As we are all mothers of young children with little free time, it has encouraged us to make time and keep our brains ticking over.*

For some men children are also the spur. An all-male group started nine years ago, 'following a discussion blaming our young children for our lack of time available for reading'. Some men are clearly very keen on reading groups; one man claims to have belonged to twelve reading groups, and we have had requests from men asking if we can find groups for them—in some cases because their wives won't let them join theirs. We have heard from two men's groups which have started in London in the past two years, professional men in their forties and fifties, some of them distinguished journalists. They say they enjoy the 'intellectual stimulation and conviviality'. Reasons why men start or join vary from 'I don't read anymore!' to:

— One night in the pub a small group of men was challenged by some female members of an existing book group that 'men could never organize a book group'. The small group (three of us) invited some friends and hence our group was formed.

We asked about the average age of group members, and again it was no surprise to learn that a third of the groups had members all in their forties, and another third's members were all 50-plus (Table 6). A very few groups have members all in their twenties—they had read about reading groups in *Cosmo*—and 20 per cent are in their thirties. We were particularly struck by the 12 per cent of groups whose membership embraces a wide age-span. In one group ages range from 27 to 84; others span from 30 to well over 90. Not many social gatherings do this, and perhaps less so now than in the past. Wide age-range seems to be a particularly strong feature in rural groups, especially the longer-established ones. Work-based groups can also range widely with members in their early twenties to late fifties, a feature they say they appreciate.

The youngest group we have come across is the 8- and 9-year-old boys and girls who wanted a group because their mothers had one. Their best book to date is Philip Pullman's *The Firework-Maker's Daughter* ('not too hard and not too easy'), and their list of what they enjoy includes the familiar 'I like it because it lets you read books you have never heard of before', as well as advantages particular to their age: 'I'm allowed more than one friend round at my house'. Lunchtime and after-hours groups are catching on in secondary schools; this is an expanding field. In the UK 30 per cent of local authorities and 37 per cent of secondary schools now run reading groups specifically designed for children and teen-agers.[4] Anne-Marie Tarter, an American who has lived in Britain for the last twenty years, is the school librarian at Ripon grammar school in north Yorkshire, and leads three groups there for a variety of ages. Books, which are some-times bought and sometimes borrowed from North York-shire Public Libraries, may be linked to a film which the group go and see together; or perhaps there will be a tie-in such as the recent Anne Frank travelling exhibition. All-night sleep-ins and reading round a theme have also gone well; the drive is to engage reluctant readers, scientists perhaps not used to reading for pleasure. The sixth-form group meets in a pizzeria, and an 'unexpected spin-off' has been the develop-ment of social skills, as 17- and 18-year-olds sit over a meal and engage in adult conversation. Fifty young people turned up for the launch of the teenage reading group (trg*) at Camberwell, south London, in 1997. Southwark Libraries now run three trg*s as well as the three family reading groups, which started in 1995. Jerry Hurst, pioneer and champion of the Southwark groups, describes trg* sessions as

— *hectic and very very noisy; trg* members are obviously not there just for the books but amongst everything else, books are enthu-siastically discussed and recommended (or otherwise) and this happens quite naturally, in a social setting of their own making.*[5]

Teenage groups are also doing well in Essex County Libraries, one of them a group run by the teenagers them-selves. Sally Brown, the children's librarian, agrees with Jerry Hurst that 'it's very much a matter of listening to the kids to see what they want'. A discussion about likes and dislikes is vital, and chocolate and crisps 'very necessary'.

The oldest group in terms of its members' age that we know of is the group run by ex-government minister Edwina Currie at Nightingale House, a large Jewish residential home for the elderly in south-west London. Hooked on Books (the name devised by one of its members) is organized by Currie together with the leisure services manager and meets every six weeks. The fifteen-strong group is all-female by joint decision; the women thought they might be inhibited by a male presence (I doubt it). They are all in their nineties or late eighties; the oldest is 97. Physically frail they may be—they wheeled, zimmered, and hobbled in—but their minds are razor-sharp and the atmosphere is electric. This is partly due to Currie's energy, but also to the sense that this is a special occasion. One member commented, 'Just because maybe you can't see or hear too well, you still want to read, to talk.' Guest speakers are a feature of the group. Currie has organized visits from an impressive galaxy of writers, including Graham Swift, Beryl Bainbridge, Ruth Rendell, and Deborah Moggach. The afternoon I was there P. D. James was talking about her book *Original Sin*. She spoke for an hour with great good humour, giving every question much thought, speaking candidly and coping tactfully with those who couldn't hear well. Currie read some extracts out; most had read the book. Members followed P. D. James's words closely, murmuring appreciatively and finishing her sentences for her. Discussion often turned upon character: the importance of consistency, credibility, and depth. Currie insists that the group reads new and current books—'people can get so cut off'—and likes to introduce them to new authors. This is a group with strong likes and dislikes—the five minutes on the solecism of 'different to' was impassioned. Group members were extremely well read, in some cases fluent in four or even six languages. One woman remembered reading Dostoevsky in Russian when she was 14; another read Agatha Christie in German in the 1920s. Everyone in the group contributed to the discussion, and sometimes members had to be forcibly silenced. Currie's remark, 'We were all great readers as children weren't we?' met with loud agreement; for these women reading is a pleasure they have enjoyed for eighty or ninety years.[6]

Probably few of the women in Nightingale House went to university; and for many elderly people being in a reading group can be a breakthrough. The University of the Third Age is a key player in the UK, with its 86,000 members engaged in a 'great experiment in learning'. A U3A group brings a wealth of experience to its discussions, as a member from Orpington reported:

— *When we recently read* Mary Barton, *group members related the conditions in nineteenth-century Manchester to their own experiences of Salford over three generations, Glasgow communities, trade unions, an erudite background account of Chartism and capitalism and a discussion of the unchanged conditions for many workers now.*

Other groups of senior citizens enjoy reading and discussing poetry, plays, and novels together. 'We all look forward to Fridays immensely, carrying on a discussion on the way home too', wrote a member of the Chauntry Group in Newark; 'I am still finishing my education.'

These non-graduates are atypical; 88 per cent of the groups in the survey said that more than half their members have had some kind of higher education, whether it be at college or university, in nursing, or some other training (Table 8). This seems to be the biggest single factor which reading groups have in common. The figure is, understandably, lower for groups with older members, but only slightly, at 82 per cent. Some people were quite explicit about their desire to read and discuss books as they had at university:

— *I started the group because I wanted to discuss books I had read— a left-over from university.*

— *I wanted to finish books and take them in properly as I used to do at university, in order to discuss them with other people.*

This nostalgia probably draws on an idealized seminar of the memory where everyone has read the book and is eager to join in the debate. Others aren't interested in going back to school or college, as they put it:

— *We don't want it to feel like studying.*

— *It's deliberately not like school.*

These graduates may not have studied literature at university, though a maths graduate says you can always spot the ones who've done English. But the working literary world is well represented. Translators, agents, novelists, journalists, and editors all enjoy reading groups. So do publishers; one explained:

— *It would be easy to let other publishers' books pass me by.*

Teachers are also keen, their interest sometimes partly professional:

— *I wanted to form the group to lead students in the school to form their own groups, and to promote links between subject areas.*

But pleasure comes into it too. The staff reading group at Ripon grammar school is known affectionately as the Dead Teachers Society:

— *We meet once a term over a Chinese meal around a big circular table and discuss a book that the group has chosen to read that term. . . . a chance to discuss something other than teaching and school!*

Higher education can prove a poor environment for general reading groups (as opposed to special-interest or literary societies): groups have faltered and failed in at least three universities and colleges. But new groups spring into life as researchers, academics, and consultants see the benefits of pooling knowledge and exchanging information and ideas across their usual discipline boundaries, 'reading by proxy' in the words of Julie Trottier of the Environmental Change Institute and founder of the Water Reading Group in Oxford. We have also found that non-graduates can be particularly determined in their approach. Six women in a rural area with no higher education between them (four in part-time work, one full-time, and 'one drone') have been meeting weekly for four years to read their way through Dostoevsky, George Eliot, and James Joyce, as well as Margaret Atwood and Frank McCourt.

More than two-thirds of the groups (67 per cent) say that over half of them are doing paid work of some kind (Table 9). Part-time work is mentioned in all age-ranges. In the lower age-ranges are women on career breaks, at home with babies and small children. What is more surprising is the number of women with full-time jobs and family commitments who are nevertheless devoted to their reading groups and determined to make room for them. For these women, the reading group is a high priority, straight after work and family:

— *I enjoy talking with other women. Most of us are working mothers, so this is an indulgence for us.*

'Up till one in the morning with the Book of Job', commented another group of working mothers after a recent meeting; 'no stopping us now.' I visited a group of women in their early thirties, busy lawyers now starting families (the latest arrival, at 6 weeks old, attended the meeting). They were planning their annual trip away, and had no intention of sacrificing their group on the altar of motherhood.

We asked some groups whether members belonged to other groups and societies: one rural group listed nineteen before running out of space and into 'etc. etc.' Could we say, then, that reading groups are for people who like joining things, whether it's a board of school governors or a choir? Or that they are for people who like learning things—evening classes often appear on the list of 'other societies'? This is partly true, and the good showing of local history societies on the lists is another reminder of the neighbourhood loyalties of reading groups. Organizing the reading group is seen by one woman as 'more satisfying than any other contribution I might make to village life'. Older women mention voluntary work commitments; a younger woman comments: 'I wanted a place to discuss and think, and no one goes to political meetings any more.'

Groups were asked whether they lived in urban, suburban, or rural areas (Table 3). We have heard from groups all over the country, from Lostwithiel in Cornwall to the Orkney Islands off the north coast of Scotland. Given the fact that most people in the UK live in towns or suburbs, the figure in our survey of 36 per cent for rural groups seems high. Is there any correlation between location and age? Rural groups tend to have older members, but also members whose ages cover a wide span (Table 6). Their timetables have to be flexible to accommodate, for example, the woman who hunts three times a week for parts of the year. A rural respondent attributes the success of reading groups in the country to the lack of other diversions:

— *In a village like this many welcome the intellectual stimulation.*

Members come from a thirty-mile radius to a group in Wiltshire, which is unusual in having a paid leader (the group grew out of an extra-mural class). One of the members does the organizing and feels that reading groups have had relatively little attention in the media until recently, despite their longevity, because of their rural bias, and

— *Country people just get on with things.*

A group in north Norfolk enjoys its summer meetings in a 'beach hut or quayside lookout overlooking creek and mudflats'. The long winter evenings on Orkney are a factor for one of the groups there, which draws its members from a fifteen-mile radius, and is a mixture of 'ferryloupers and Orcadians', incomers and established residents. This mix, common to many rural groups, can make for interesting dynamics.

For communities who may feel cut off, the reading group has much to offer. It has a part to play in day centres for the blind, secure mental hospitals, and prisons. The National Library for the Blind is involved in research projects on reading groups for the visually impaired; their Reading Advice manager thinks that groups of sighted and non-sighted readers work best, and is keen to address the need for the visually impaired to have access to 'what everyone else reads, at the same time'. This can be difficult. Large print and audio book choices can be a bit conservative, 'but we did get a Booker Prize into Braille within two days of winning'.[7] Reading groups in prison are being encouraged in the UK by initiatives in reader development, involving readers in residence.[8] In America prison reading groups have had a more formalized function. The Changing Lives through Literature reading and discussion programmes give offenders the choice of being 'sentenced to literature and probation instead of prison'. In the opinion of the leader of one such group, 'Literature helps these men to see that there are many perspectives on an event, many interpretations of a story.'[9] These American groups seem to read a lot of fiction, whereas the group which I facilitate in a men's prison outside London likes to mix fiction and non-fiction. The men, whose ages range from early twenties to late fifties, choose the books themselves, pay £1 towards them, and keep them afterwards. We meet once a month for an hour. Choosing is an important part of the process, and our first choice, *Angela's Ashes*, proved the right book to start with, and not just because of the identification with the impoverished upbringing. Like all other groups, they like to read what everyone else is reading, and follow the progress of bestsellers like *Angela's Ashes* in the media. Hence the choice of Harry Potter. Opinion veered towards and then away ('it's a children's book') and then back towards with the hype surrounding the next in the series.

Reading groups in prisons are not new of course. The solace of communal reading was vouched for by an inmate of Kingsbench Prison in 1826: 'My pretty Jane has, alternatively with her not less lively sister Julia, cheated the otherwise dull and lingering hours of winter evenings, by reading aloud *The Ladies' Museum* [the magazine he is writing to] to their mother and myself.'[10] Elizabeth Fry's prison reading groups were famous. The fashionable, the great, and the good flocked to witness her reading with women prisoners in the early nineteenth century: 'The American Ambassador wrote home to say that he had now seen the two greatest sights of London—St Paul's Cathedral, and Mrs Fry reading to the prisoners in Newgate.... "Tears flowed freely from eyes which perhaps had never shed such tears till then."' For the prisoners the event was, Fry's biographer observes, 'a theatre and a concert, a church and a superior family circle, all rolled into one'.[11]

The variety so characteristic of reading groups appears in the different ways that they get started. Skittles teams and aerobics classes have transformed themselves into reading groups, as have choirs, friends from a rambling club, and a group who met on a short residential course and wanted to continue meeting regularly. The records of a book club in Stockton in the north of England, which I have in my possession, show that the twelve men started their club in June 1776 as a 'friendly Society or Monthly Clubb [*sic*] for the Promoting, easy and chearful, but liberal Conversation; mutual Entertainment and literary Improvement'; their first rule: 'The Meetings to be held at the Black Lyon, Robert Bamborough's and Robert Coates's alternately, on the second Friday in each Month'. A few months later, in February 1777, the society decided to become a book club, with each member contributing 2s. 6d. ($12\frac{1}{2}$ p) a quarter to buy books. They started with Voltaire's *Candide* and a *Life of Voltaire*, and took in the *Monthly Review*, a lot of biography and history, and a good selection of classics in translation. In the 1780s they were reading more Voltaire (sixteen volumes), Adam Smith, Dr Johnson, Boswell, Ann Yearsley's poems, and a book on gardening, but no novels.

Given the high number of all-women groups, it's no surprise to find that many of them had their origins in women's organizations such as the Women's Institute, the Townswomen's Guild, the National Women's Register (formerly the National Housewives' Register), groups for university wives, and post-natal groups. A twenty-three-year-old group in a rural area started through baby clinics and playgroups:

— *We are a bit legendary in the area and probably seen as elitist, though I don't think we are. Apart from being a book club, we have acted as support group for each other and have seen each other through births, divorces, marriages, deaths and degrees . . . Our children have the advantage of having grown up with thirteen mothers, a fact they really appreciate. We all know we can rely on each other (catering a speciality—we have done weddings and funerals for each other). I know that some of our husbands think the group is a very formidable force.*

Mixed groups have started in the workplace and school staffrooms, also via university networks, and out of evening classes and Workers' Educational Association (WEA) groups; the class finishes but the group goes on. Public libraries are the venue for groups starting up in Yorkshire, in an initiative new to the UK, bibliotherapy. The RAYS

Project (The Reading And You Scheme) is a partnership between cultural services and local GP practices, which uses reading groups to help patients 'affected by mild depression, stress or anxiety, or who are socially isolated'.

Sometimes the impetus to start a group may spring from the books, or even book. More than one discussion of A. S. Byatt's *Possession* has grown into a reading group, one at a party, one from an animated conversation round the photocopying machine at work. Another group say they were 'fed up with snatched book discussions at work'. The need to talk about what she had just read propelled one respondent:

— *I initiated the group from a need to discuss immediately after reading, with people from divers perspectives.*

Most of the groups in the survey mention friends, neighbours, or family as the main starting-point:

— *I started it because a friend belonged to a reading group and I thought it sounded a lovely idea. I asked friends who enjoyed books to join.*

— *I asked a friend and she spread the word.*

— *A group of people who use the same shop.*

— *I put a brief article in the parish mag. and then mentioned it to a few people I knew were readers.*

— *I put out an email and started the group at work; we meet in the company learning centre.*

— *My daughter set it up by inviting friends with similar interests to join. I was included!*

— *We started in a wine bar when our children left junior school.*

— *Three friends discussed the idea and then invited two or three friends each.*

These may well be people who don't all know each other. Sometimes a piece in a newspaper or magazine has got someone going: 'If French and Saunders can do it so can we'. This is a reference to the comedians Dawn French and Jennifer Saunders, and the Orange promotion in 1997. This got a lot of groups started, as did the *YOU* scheme:

— *I first read about reading groups in the* Mail on Sunday*'s* YOU *magazine in January 1998 and decided I wanted to become a member of a reading group. I made enquiries on the island (Isle of Wight) to no avail so I decided to start my own. I placed a small ad in the local free weekly newspaper and made posters which were placed in local libraries, bookshops, and post offices. All members (age from mid-twenties to late fifties, only women replied) were new to each other from the outset. Each member pays £1 per meeting towards refreshments. We have a contact with a local bookseller who gives us a discount of £1 off per book purchased.*

Advertisements in local papers have caught the eyes of newcomers:

— *I was new to the area and looking for 'like-minded' people to get to know and something to fill my evenings.*

Some enthusiasts bring the idea with them, perhaps from abroad, maybe from one of the expatriate groups which do so well. Or they may have friends or relations in groups overseas: groups in France, Italy, America, South Africa, and Australia are all cited as inspiring groups here. Inspiration and contact too—groups all over the world swap information with each other, and like to keep in touch.

Some of the overseas groups we heard from were told about our survey by friends in groups in this country. It's a global word-of-mouth network, and adds powerfully to our portrait of the reading-group movement as something highly active and interactive.

Three

How Groups Choose and What They Read

'We all have an equal say.'

How do groups choose what to read? The answer in most cases is 'with difficulty'. 'As democratically as possible' is a major imperative, and this can take time and effort. On some of our visits to groups we have been struck by the way they can take almost as long choosing what to read next as they do discussing this month's book.[1] So it is obviously an important part of the meeting,

— *often as interesting as the book discussion,*

and after seventeen years it isn't necessarily any easier:

— *We have read quite a variety of books over the years and our biggest problem now is always 'what do we read next?' We have tried to deal with it in different ways e.g. nineteenth-century authors, South American writers, themes such as parent/child, personal recommendations. We cut lists from the newspapers and pick up leaflets from bookshops, but it is still quite difficult to organize several months ahead.*

The groups in our survey have devised a dazzling array of ingenious methods; and choosing how you choose can be another minefield:

— *It's taken a long time to sort this out.*

Some are happy to abdicate responsibility to an outside agent, such as the *Mail on Sunday*'s *YOU* reading-group selection:

— *We do not want any individual to choose a book, because of the responsibility of others liking it.*
— *To have the books chosen for us means that no one takes the blame if the meeting falls flat.*
— *Through the YOU choices we sometimes read books we are unlikely to choose ourselves.*
— *YOU gives us the opportunity to read authors one would not necessarily pick off the shelf.*

However, half those who use the *YOU* selections and discounts also like to pick their own books occasionally—a symptom of the reading group's need to assert its own identity. Library-based groups who borrow their books depend upon the sets provided by the librarians, but the group can usually make suggestions, or choose from an annotated list. Groups who buy their books—the majority in our survey— usually have a paperback-only rule, and sometimes a length rule too:

— *Exceptionally long books are out, because of the busy lives of some of the members.*

— *The number of pages should be entered on the proposal sheet (also price), to be taken into account when voting.*

— *Must be in paperback with at least two copies in the County Library.*

Groups have invented an assortment of strategies for choosing:

— *Each person takes a turn to nominate a book and there is no discussion.*

— *Alphabetical order of surnames in the group.*

— *We have a meeting once a year where we choose one book from each member's suggestions of three books they have heard about.*

— *Suggestions recorded during the year and in November each member has eleven votes and the top eleven listed are picked. Members then offer to 'present' a book and the programme for the year is settled.*

— *Each participant chooses two books and gives names to the two members compiling the list; these two create an interesting list. The two members who compile the list are different each time, taking turns.*

— *Sometimes one book leads to another (e.g. Rose Tremain's* The Way I Found Her *led us to* Le Grand Meaulnes).

— The Taming of the Shrew *emerged as a natural choice from Germaine Greer's comments on it.*

— *Consensus, experiment.*

— *Try to gain a consensus. Usual problem is someone suggests something, everyone else says that sounds OK but without much conviction. It generally needs one other person to sound convinced to sway the crowd.*

— *We have a planning meeting in June (ready for holiday reading); bring two to three books each and talk briefly about them; spread them on the floor and debate which ten to choose. Some are voted immediately, the remainder get fought over.*

— *We each make one 'anonymous' suggestion on a piece of paper in a box every ten months. The selection is those ten in the order out of the box.*

— *Usually a shouting match.*

— *We have a list but there is usually a certain amount of argument.*

— *A bit like the election of the Pope—just happens following suggestions.*

— *An inner sanctum chooses.*

— *We have a leader (unpaid) who chooses from our suggestions.*

— *The host for the evening chooses without reference to the other members and buys eight books to be revealed at the end of the evening. The highlight of each evening is 'what new book will we be taking away with us?'*

The principles guiding choice might be to do with the books. We have come across a few specialized groups who read only crime fiction or classics. An eleven-year-old group started by members of the same synagogue choose 'author or subject of Jewish interest (for example C. P. Snow, George Eliot)'. And indeed, think of an author you like and there's probably a group for him or her, either a literary society or a website. Literary societies are a type of reading group, and boast a flourishing and impressive range, from Lascelles Abercrombie to Charlotte M. Yonge.[2] (A fictional Yonge society takes centre stage, murderously, in Harriet Waugh's 1997 novel *A Chaplet of Pearls*.) Many have a long history. About 200 people, including George Bernard Shaw, joined the London

Browning Society when it was founded in 1881, though others turned up their noses. 'They praise Browning's poetry chiefly because they believe they alone understand it', grumbled Andrew Lang. As Browning societies proliferated throughout England's provincial towns, Ellen Terry objected: 'These societies have terrorized the ordinary reader into letting Browning alone.'[3] Shakespeare societies and clubs were also popular in the second half of the nineteenth century, and women joined enthusiastically. The Coterie was one such club, founded by black women in Kansas in 1889.[4] For these groups an early 'how to' literature sprang up, with publications like L. M. Griffiths's *Evenings with Shakspere* [*sic*], *a Handbook containing special help for Shakspere Societies dedicated to lady-members of the Clifton Shakspere Society*. And beside Shakespeare, the Bible: Bible-reading groups form what must be the largest family of reading groups, with the longest history and the most variegated siblings.

The Good Book is not alone in inspiring one-book groups. My own reading group is currently reading *Little Dorrit* an instalment at a time, over the eighteen months it originally took to appear. Reading Dickens in real time gives us some idea of what it felt like to be his first readers, reading aloud to each other, commenting, and speculating on what's coming next. We have been surprised to see how little Dickens depends on cliff-hangers and suspense to keep us going. In America it's Proust who is enjoying the solo spotlight, much to the amusement of the French press: 'On trouve des cercles proustiens même dans les coins les plus reculés du pays.' The members of the Marcel Proust Support Group in San Francisco pledged to read ten pages a day, holding their bi-monthly meetings in fin-de-siècle venues (Café Proust, madeleines 75 cents apiece). 'Les prousto-philes', observes a French journalist, 'sortent du bois.'[5]

Back in the UK, James Joyce is responsible for the slowest group we have come across: the London University (Charles Peake) Seminar for Research into James Joyce's *Ulysses*, founded by Professor Andrew Gibson, has read five chapters in fourteen years. They get through a couple of pages an evening, reading aloud two or three sentences at a time, then pausing to discuss them: 'It's mainly for academics, postgraduates, and London Joycean scholars, though non-academics and international Joyceans drop in.' The dozen or so Joyceans meet monthly and range in age from the mid-twenties to late sixties; they organize and speak at confer-ences and have published three collections of essays. The all-important decision about which chapter to go for next (they don't work systematically through the book) is 'becoming more democratic' with the passing years. Joyce is clearly a reading-group-friendly author; he inspired one of the most original groups in our survey, formed twenty years ago in Boston, Mass.

— *for the purpose of reading the one James Joyce few can crack on their own, and also because it must be heard as well as read. We meet perhaps eight times a year, each 'Finnegan' having the meeting at their house. Buffet dinner is followed by reading aloud, one or two pages a person . . . we are more like a chamber music ensemble than a book discussion group. . . . It took us five years to finish the* Wake *and we began again (as Joyce instructs). Since then we have read a variety of things, and abandoned not a few. We thought to read* Ulysses *in tandem with* The Odyssey *but found they didn't track, so read them both separately.*

They have done well with Shakespeare but failed with Byron's *Don Juan*:

— *There is now a sort of rule that apart from the* Wake *(which we begin again every so often) we read works intended to be read aloud.*

Six of the thirteen members have Irish roots; the group includes two journalists, a book critic, an arts editor and poet, a banker, a public servant who paints, a photographer, a novelist and several aspiring novelists, and two dogs— Finnegan and Earwicker.

Most groups, however, like a varied diet and have ideas about how to get it.

— *We try to achieve a balance, considering such factors as the gender of the author, fact/fiction, literature of other countries/ cultures, an occasional classic or sometimes a poet.*

— *Never read the same author twice.*

— *We alternate old favourites and recently published books.*

— *We alternate 'modern'/classic.*

— *Books we have always wanted to read but haven't got round to.*

— *We have deliberately chosen books from other countries— India, Japan, Africa, Russia, Germany, France etc.*

— *The death of a well-known author sometimes triggers interest.*

— *Sometimes there will be a theme, e.g. books about India or by Indian authors, books in translation, family sagas, books about the sea (this was very successful and included* Moby-Dick, *Golding's* Rites of Passage, *and Conrad).*

— *Sometimes a theme, e.g. adultery, utopian writing; or a Booker list, and choose our winner.*

— *We have tried themes, e.g. humour, historical, but not found this successful.*

— *We decided to read as many of the three books about the kidnapping and hostage situation as we had time for (Keenan's* An Evil Cradling, *McCarthy and Morrell's* Some Other Rainbow *and Waite's* Taken on Trust*), and it was really interesting to compare not only their different interpretations of the same experience, but also the different writing styles.*

A pattern can develop without apparent forethought:

— *Sometimes a theme emerges and we explore it. We dart about, but definitely want to include literature that keeps us in touch with contemporary writing.*

— *For a while a recurrent theme seemed to be lost babies— interesting that male authors shared this theme; also interesting how differently each author used the idea.*

Groups sometimes find a cure for the 'desperation' mentioned once or twice by seeking outside help:

— *The man from the local bookshop brings a selection of books to our meeting about every six months. He gives a brief talk on the books. This is our most popular meeting.*

— *Borrow books from a local bookstore, look at them at July meeting to plan the next year.*

— *We started from a list published in* Cosmo *of 'The World's 50 Best Novels'.*

— *We keep book reviews and take them along to meetings.*

— *Prize nomination lists, articles in journals, TLS, supplements, etc.*

— *One of the benefits of the group has been the development of awareness of possible reading-group material in each of us. We all listen more acutely to books described on radio and television and in the newspapers.*

— *We used often to choose from the Booker list, but have so often been disappointed in recent years that we don't bother as much now, but go more on reviews and personal recommendations.*

Personal recommendation via word of mouth, the favoured communication system of the reading group, works well for choice. Ideas come from family, friends, and work colleagues, or from what has gone well in another group. Two cousins who live at a distance remember to put their reading lists in their handbags so they can swap suggestions when they meet. With time, groups work out what suits them best.

— *We've learnt not to be too ambitious and to know something concrete about a book choice before selecting it.*

— *We find that our choice now reflects our real preferences—we are less likely to try and be 'clever'.*

— *We plan our programme annually now instead of choosing from month to month.*

— *Have tried two methods: (1) each person suggests two books and speaks briefly about them—one of us makes a list—we then vote for six or seven novels. (It nearly always works out to be one from each person); recently (2) at each meeting one person suggests two or three possibilities, which the rest of the group choose from, which becomes the book for the next meeting. This allows us to feel more spontaneous and not sticking loyally to a list which was started perhaps a year ago.*

Putting books in pairs can pay off: Arabella Weir's *Does my Bum Look Big in This?* beside Germaine Greer's *The Female Eunuch*; a novel by Scott Fitzgerald next to a biography of Zelda. Practical considerations can be important:

— *We choose last year's Booker because the library has plenty of copies*

as can social ones:

— *If there's a film just out, we read the book and have a night out. Or get the video.*

Sometimes groups may want to set some rules:

— *You must have read the book before you propose it.*
— *One of our unwritten rules is that you shouldn't have read the book before choosing it.*
— *Must cost under £10.00.*

And some just get stuck, as a member of a 30-something Californian group lamented:

— *I do wish we had a better system for picking better books— we're working on it—some real stinkers have crept in, though.*

Although groups can spend ages choosing, they may finally pick books no one knows much about. Risk-taking and flying blind may be part of the pleasure. Groups we have visited have plumped for books they 'like the sound of', or have seen people reading on the tube. Children can inspire indirectly:

— *We read* Trainspotting *because our sons and daughters were reading it. Led to lively discussion and very diverse opinions.*
— *We chose* The Beach *to see what our offspring are up to. Raised lots of issues.*

One of the main determinants seems to be the desire to read what one reading-group member describes as 'live books', and one of the most frequently mentioned pleasures is to do with choice:

— *I enjoy reading books I wouldn't necessarily choose—the opening sentence of* The Ice People *would have put off 100 per cent of our group had it not been selected.*

— *Most of us have been pleasantly surprised by an unexpected choice.*

— *Some I would never have read before were actually the most memorable, e.g.* Zen and the Art of Motorcycle Maintenance.

— *Nobody had heard of Bulgakov's* The Master and Margarita *so came to it without preconceptions and unanimously admired and enjoyed it.*

Wanting to be stretched is one of the most frequently given reasons for starting or joining a group:

— *Our reading was getting safe.*

— *I was stuck on historical romances.*

— *We want to expand our reading horizons.*

— *An incentive to read books we wouldn't otherwise try.*

— *To make us read authors we otherwise might not (gets us out of the loop).*

— *A good idea to introduce myself to new books.*

— *Reading stuff we wouldn't otherwise touch.*

Even a book that's disliked has its function:

— *Although many people have disliked some of the books, the general view is that we joined in order to extend our range of reading, and therefore read whatever comes.*

Whatever comes: one of the areas we wanted to investigate was, of course, what groups read. So we asked about categories of books, whether the sex of the author was an important factor, and for a list of books which groups had read recently. The first thing to strike us about this long list of 2,816 books was its enormous variety. Between them, 284 groups listed 698 authors and 1,160 different titles.[6] Only four of the titles had been read by more than fifty of the 284 groups, and three-quarters of the titles were one-offs, i.e. read by only one group (see Table 14). And what a range, from the diary of an eighteenth-century farmer's wife to *White Merc with Fins*, from Aeschylus and Amis (M. and K.) to Zangwill, Zahavi, and Zola. Cervantes, Dante, and Chaucer are there, as well as Patti Smith and Bridget Jones. Many groups have read books in all the categories we asked about (Table 10):

Fiction, contemporary
Fiction, twentieth-century
Fiction, pre-twentieth-century
Non-fiction, biography, memoirs
Poetry
Other

A very few groups read only poetry, and enjoy developing a theme, period, or poet. Some like to start or end their meeting with a poem, or to have a special poetry evening, perhaps at Christmas. There were fifty-one entries for poetry, from Pam Ayres and John Betjeman to Derek Walcott and William Wordsworth. Four groups have read T. S. Eliot's *The Waste Land* recently, though not always successfully:

— *We felt it was really something to be studied in depth, more for students than reading group members.*

Ted Hughes's *Birthday Letters* was read by fourteen groups, and other work by Hughes by a further eight. For some, *Birthday Letters* was an unexpected hit:

— *Everyone agreed that it had been difficult but extremely rewarding; it sparked an intense and fascinating discussion.*

Seamus Heaney's poetry went down well with another group:

— *This proved to some who 'didn't like poetry' that it was explicable, entertaining and moving although it didn't necessarily 'rhyme'.*

A very few groups read only plays; more choose plays or play-reading to add occasional variety; thirty-five plays were listed. Four groups had read Shakespeare recently; one group enjoyed reading *King Lear* alongside Jane Smiley's *A Thousand Acres*. 'Other' categories mentioned include gardening, travel, children's books, letters and diaries, cookery books, science fiction and crime, humorous books, magazine articles and reviews, and a cassette recording of a radio play (*Spoonface Steinberg*). With a few notable exceptions, biography and autobiography come off poorly:

— *We all found Denis Healey's* The Time of My Life *to contain a list of people and names, to have no real depth to it—it made for very tedious reading.*

— *Biography of Frederick Ashton badly received; too society-driven, too much name-dropping.*

— Aristocrats—*too much recorded speech.*

— Georgiana, Duchess of Devonshire—*nobody liked it.*

One group I visited were considering reading Margaret Forster's biography of Daphne du Maurier—their first book had
been *Jamaica Inn*—but on the whole they judged most biographies as too long for them. Of current biographers, Claire
Tomalin did best, with eleven entries; three groups mentioned *Mrs Jordan's Profession* as going particularly well.
For one of the groups reading this book, we had the benefit
of seeing individual returns and a glimpse of internal dis-
agreement: one person found the book 'tedious', while for
another it was 'a surprise find and wonderful book'.

We asked groups if they read more books by men or by
women, and if the sex of the author was an important factor.
A small band of all-female groups has chosen to read only
female authors, and a gay group we heard from picks books
by men with a gay interest—though they admit to wearying
recently of 'yet another depressing novel about AIDS'. Many
all-women groups think that the gender of the author influ-
ences their choice, sometimes away from male authors:

— We avoid books for men by men.

— More by women. We are aware of this and are actively looking for
   male authors with appeal—it's hard.

— Mostly women—it is an issue apparently—we prefer women and
   make ourselves read men.

Do men and women read differently? We compared male and
female groups by gender of author, and found that more
women read books by men than men read books by women
(Table 12). But not a great deal more: 53 per cent of the books
all-female groups read are by men, whereas 36 per cent of the
books male groups read are by women, i.e. about a third of
the books men read are by women, and women read about

half and half. This was a more even spread than we expected, especially given the conclusions drawn from a survey carried out in March 2000 for the Orange Prize for Fiction by Book Marketing Ltd. This research analysed the reactions of 200 respondents to the cover designs and titles of twenty books (not their contents), and claimed that 'women fail to seduce male readers': 'While 40 per cent of women surveyed said they would read books they believed appealed mainly to men, only 25 per cent of men said they would consider a book they felt was for women.' But do these figures, which are not dissimilar from ours, prove that 'Men are far more biased towards books written by men than women are to books written by women'? A bit more biased perhaps—but research on judging a book by its cover may be of more use to cover designers than anyone else. Interestingly, the overwhelming majority of groups in our survey agree either that the sex is not important, or that they like to strike a balance.

— *Equal—not that it's not important; make a conscious effort.*

— *Sex not important except appreciating our male member may not wish to read books aimed at women and which tend to be by women.*

— *Sex not important—ideas are.*

Men are generally thought to read less fiction than women, and the all-male groups in our survey—we only had a small number in this category—do pick slightly more non-fiction, biography in particular. Though not uncritically: Michael Heseltine in Michael Crick's version was succinctly dismissed by one group as 'a boring opportunist'. Another all-male group mentions going for 'lots of Roth'. And while women are choosing male authors, they aren't always enjoying them. Some of the lads get the thumbs down:

— Fever Pitch—*what a moaner, oh for heaven's sake grow up we all said— except for one male and one young girl.*

— High Fidelity—*over-hyped, and one-joke book which no one liked.*

— *Martin Amis's* Money—*vulgar and distasteful.*

— *Kingsley Amis—curmudgeonly.*

Mixed groups notice gender divisions:

— Snow Falling on Cedars *was generally preferred by the men in the group.*

— *We have two male members: this stops us making too many sweeping generalizations about men. In reading* Larry's Party *where there is a male protagonist it was very useful to have two male viewpoints. One man was the same age as Larry and so identified with the eras he lived through. As a woman I felt surely men are more insightful than Larry and was prepared to criticize Carol Shields for this portrayal until one of the male group members said he thought men were generally less insightful! An enlightening but depressing moment.*

We looked at the nationality of the authors being read, to see if British groups like to read within home shores or venture further afield (Table 11). About half the books are British and a quarter American, with very little being read in translation. These figures remain fairly constant whether the groups are urban, suburban, or rural; rural groups read slightly more British writers. The more striking variations signal regional and local associations. Groups in Scotland favour Scottish writers; Lake District groups choose books with Lake

District connections. Local authors do well, especially if they are willing, as quite a few are, to visit groups in the area. A group in Devon picks writing with rural links: Ted Hughes's 'Raincharm for the Duchy', Frank Muir's *A Kentish Lad*, Ronald Blythe's *Akenfield*. This last went badly in an urban group, but proved a good choice for another rural group:

— *Accounts from people of different occupations and lifestyles living in a rural community something like our own. Some of us are relative newcomers to this town, five to ten years, where others were born in the neighbourhood and could relate to the accounts given in the book; an interesting and entertaining discussion.*

The strong sense of place and community is a recognizable reading-group characteristic, sometimes developed to the level of expertise:

— *I have just organized the group and friends to read and review about thirty/forty books by Hampshire authors as part of a display put on by the local library.*

A neighbourhood can also create a hot spot: a number of groups around Oxford were reading Jenny Diski's *Skating to Antarctica* at the time of the survey, but it appears on very few other lists.

Do groups go exclusively for the latest books, or do they spread their reading across the centuries? We looked at the date of first publication for the books they have been reading recently (Table 13). Over a third (39 per cent) of the books were first published between 1996 and 1999; the low figure for 1999 is due to the fact that most groups read only paperbacks, and most books first published in 1999 won't be in paperback until 2000. About two-thirds of the books (64 per cent) are from the 1990s; the 1970s and the 1980s see a slump in interest. Whether we sort the groups by age or type of area, the distribution remains more or less constant. Groups with a wide age-range like nineteenth-century literature, and so do the under-30s—but this last category is very small. The nineteenth century is as popular as the first half of the twentieth century, with the great nineteenth-century novel holding its own: Dickens, Austen, Eliot, James, Hardy, Edith Wharton, and Wilkie Collins are all in the top fifty authors, though Trollope didn't make it (Table 15).

The most popular category by far is contemporary fiction, though within this area there are some very strongly expressed likes and dislikes—reading groups voice both with equal force. The bulk of the titles are what booksellers call literary fiction. Richard Todd, author of *Consuming Fictions: The Booker Prize and Fiction in Britain Today*, attributes 'the extraordinary energy that has transformed literary fiction in Britain into a truly global literature since . . . the early 1980s' to the impact of the Booker and other prizes.[7] It is certainly true that groups all over the world mention being guided in their choices by prizes and shortlists. Non-enthusiasts for reading groups sometimes condemn their diet as middle-brow; is this either fair or useful? I think it is fair to say that literary elites and establishments have always defined themselves against the middlebrow. 'If any human being, man, woman, dog, cat or half-crushed worm dares call me "middle-brow"', wrote Virginia Woolf in a letter she did not send to the *New Statesman*, 'I will take my pen and stab him, dead.'[8] Reading groups, though, are often reading the same serious literary fiction (for example Atwood, McEwan, Morrison) as those literature departments which show so little interest in their activities; and their discussions aren't so different from those in the seminar rooms either—and often better prepared. And when I hear from three different groups in one evening, with *Nicholas Nickleby*, *Lady Chatterley's Lover*, and José Saramago's *Siege of Lisbon* as their current books, I have to conclude that 'middlebrow' is not a helpful label to describe this reading.

Contemporary literary fiction tops the list then, with lighter fare foundering badly. James Michener's *The Drifters* was seen off as a 'dud book' by a group of successful professional women, and genre fiction also gets poor ratings. Crime fiction, courtroom dramas, and romantic fiction have been judged too lightweight, affording too little to discuss. 'We have joked about Elmore Leonard for years', commented an American group on a bad choice. Groups also develop a sense of what they won't get on with:

— *We have learnt to steer clear of magic realism.*

— *We find non-fiction difficult to discuss.*

There are other pitfalls too:

— *Illyrian Spring by Ann Bridge went badly. This was an old favourite of an elderly member and was no longer in print. Favourite books tend to inhibit open discussion as people may hesitate to criticize the work.*

— *We all found that some 'classics' of our youth were now very disappointing—*Vanity Fair, Lorna Doone, *the books of Sir Walter Scott. But Austen, Trollope, Hardy, Bennett are still great favourites.*

Personal enthusiasms not shared can rock the boat.

— *E. Annie Proulx's* Shipping News *went badly. The American lady who recommended it loved it and wanted to reread it with the group. She was disappointed by our lukewarm response and after several attempts to discuss the book objectively we drifted off the subject as she obviously felt beleaguered, even 'threatened'.*

— A Summer Birdcage *went badly. I was the only member who empathized with Margaret Drabble. I was most surprised at others' lack of enthusiasm.*

— Jan Morris *went badly—my choice! I loved the writing— others thought it overdone and self-conscious. I felt under attack.*

— Anne Tyler's The Accidental Tourist *was dire. It was difficult because the person who chose it, loved it. Everyone else felt they had to be diplomatic. No one liked A. S. Byatt's The Game either. But the 'chooser' acknowledged this, so it wasn't so bad.*

Individual sensitivities also have to be accommodated:

— *One member will not read beyond the first swear-word or bonking session.*

In answer to our question about books that had gone well or badly, 183 different titles were listed as going well, with the list topped by *Captain Corelli's Mandolin* and *Angela's Ashes*. 177 titles were listed as going badly, the usual reason given being that general agreement in liking/disliking the book had left the group nothing to discuss. But some strong memories were stirred:

— *We hated* Men are from Mars *and abandoned it midway through. Boring and patronizing. A few basic points expanded into a money-making exercise.*

— Jeannette Winterson's *Boating for Beginners—nothing in it, couldn't make any sense in it, author obnoxious.*

— James Joyce's *Ulysses: we hated it! It's the book at the top of everyone's best book choice and we are convinced it is because it is so often an A-level book and nobody reads anything ever again!*

We have all tried it twice and find it unreadable. In fact we have a complete complex about it.

— Lolita—*many objected to the subject.*

There were some notable disappointments:

— *Anaïs Nin's* A Spy in the House of Love, *promised erotica, delivered banality.*

On the other hand, new enthusiasms can be sparked:

— *Since we read* Hogfather *I have become a Terry Pratchett fan although I would never have dreamt of reading him normally.*

— *Kurt Vonnegut's* Breakfast of Champions *I thought was a waste of paper but the person leading the group was able to illustrate what I had been unable to appreciate.*

Groups are wary of what they call 'over-hyped' books and mark them down accordingly:

— Amsterdam *felt unworthy of Booker.*

— *We thought* Quarantine *by Jim Crace overrated, were amazed that it won a prize, and many found it hard to find anything to say.*

Arundhati Roy's *The God of Small Things*, Peter Carey's *Jack Maggs*, and Peter Hoeg's *Miss Smilla's Feeling for Snow* attracted similar opprobrium, as did Beryl Bainbridge's *Every Man for Himself:*

— *We'd heard so much hype and in the end were disappointed.*

Bainbridge turns out to be rather a controversial reading-group author. She appears forty-four times on lists of books read recently, with five different novels, so groups are reading her, but protesting as they do. Twenty-seven groups have read *Every Man for Himself*, and while a few are intrigued by the mix of fact and fiction, many more leap at the chance for a good ticking off:

— *Not one member of the group enjoyed it; in fact we all thought it was so bad that none of us wish to read Beryl Bainbridge again. We found it boring and without any substance whatsoever.*

— *We expected more as she had come second in the Booker Prize. [It won the 1996 Whitbread Novel Award.]*

— *Maybe too much* Titanic *stuff around.*

— *We hated the characters and couldn't wait for the* Titanic *to sink.*

Bainbridge seems to have inspired more vitriol than most, but in fact quite a few books, and most of the top ten, distinguished themselves as crossovers, i.e. going well in some groups and badly in others. Not that a book that goes badly is disliked:

— *Strangely enough,* Captain Corelli's Mandolin *went badly. Those of us who'd finished it all liked it so much that there was too much agreement. Two had found it very difficult to get into because of the historical detail in the first few chapters.*

Though, as so often in this survey, there is a different point of view:

— *We didn't like the style of writing. Lacked empathy with the hero and found the ending implausible.*

— *I wouldn't say it went badly, but we all thought it flawed (implausible ending) and overrated.*

This talk of *Captain Corelli* brings us inevitably to the list of reading-group favourites for 1999 (Table 16). At first glance this may look predictable, with the usual suspects at the top, and for good reason: reading groups want to be part of the reading community. But they also want to have their own identity, and reading up to a dozen books a year gives a group plenty of scope for having a book of their own—hence the huge number of titles (882) in our survey read by only one group (Table 14). And their top ten, listed for the period June–December 1999 (Table 16), bears no relation to the bestselling paperbacks of the year (most groups read, and buy, paperbacks). Maeve Binchy's *Tara Road* may top the UK bestselling paperbacks for 1999 with sales of over a million (see pages 190–1), but it was chosen by only two of the groups in our survey—putting it level with Henry James's *The Golden Bowl* and lagging far behind Ted Hughes's *Birthday Letters*. Likewise, the list of top ten writers in the *Independent*'s survey of 40,000 readers in January 2000 has only one author—Jane Austen—who also appears on the reading groups' top fifty authors.[9] There's a closer fit between our groups' top thirty authors and the most read top thirty in the Waterstone's Reading Survey of November 1999 (Table 15 and page 192). But even so they only share thirteen writers in common—that's under half. The main points of divergence are the thrillers, romances, and lighter fiction, which lack the requisite reading-group fibre.

What sorts of books and writers have made it to the reading-group top ten? The nationality mix of the authors gives the lie to accusations of parochial little Englandism. We have here four British, one Indian, one Irish, two Canadian, and two American writers. The gender division is not quite even, with six men to four women. But one of the men, Arthur Golden, is impersonating a woman, so perhaps it is even after all. This reflects the overall balance of male and female writers on the long list of all the authors read (Table 12), and is perhaps surprising, given the preponderance of women in reading groups and the generally held view that women read more female than male writers. The list has its prize-winners—Roy won the Booker, Michaels the Orange Prize, and McCourt the Pulitzer—but is low on well-established names. Only Atwood and McEwan have strong track records and backlists. Six of the ten titles are by first-time authors: McCourt, Roy, Frazier, Atkinson, Michaels, and Golden (though Michaels has published poetry and Frazier short stories and travel writing). This predilection for books from authors who are not well established is another pointer to reading groups liking to go their own way.

Only two books—*Enduring Love* and *Behind the Scenes at the Museum*—set most of their action in England. Two—*Alias Grace* and *Cold Mountain*—are set in the nineteenth century, and seven in the more recent past. Only one, *Enduring Love*, is set in the present. Groups approve of books which can extend their knowledge base:

— *We learnt a lot of history from* Birdsong *and* Captain Corelli's Mandolin.

— Memoirs of a Geisha *and* The God of Small Things *introduced us to worlds we knew nothing about.*

Common themes and patterns emerge: war and its aftermath (*Fugitive Pieces, Cold Mountain, Birdsong, Captain Corelli's Mandolin*); damaged childhood (*Behind the Scenes at the Museum, Angela's Ashes, The God of Small Things*), and the overriding importance of a strong context—there is a lot of violence of one sort or another in this top ten. They are challenging books in other ways too. Foreign words and specialized and arcane terminology are a feature of *Enduring Love, Captain Corelli's Mandolin*, and *Fugitive Pieces*: these are not always easy books to read. And whereas American groups observed in the mid-1980s had a preference for realism,[10] groups in Britain currently enjoy what they call 'poetic' novels such as *Fugitive Pieces* and *The God of Small Things*.

Another striking feature of this top ten is its tendency to mix fact and fiction and play on the boundary between the two. Groups puzzle over the appendix and references at the end of *Enduring Love* about de Clerambault's syndrome: is all this stuff fact or fiction, and does it matter? They join in on both sides of the controversy over the literal truth of McCourt's memories in *Angela's Ashes*, and they comment, sometimes with irritation, on the deliberate wrong-footing of the reader at the beginning of *Memoirs of a Geisha*. Golden opens with a 'Translator's Note' by 'Jakob Haarhuis, Arnold Rusoff Professor of Japanese History, New York University', claiming to have taken down from dictation the memoirs of a Japanese geisha. Only at the end of the book are we told that 'the character of Sayuri and her story are completely invented'.[11] Reading groups were alert to the fact/fiction issue, and some objected:

— *We all felt let down at the end, having been led to believe this was a true story.*

But it provided a lively talking point for a work-based group with their Japanese branch, and for another British group it was one of their best books:

— *We were fascinated (and at times horrified) by the exposition of this closed world and we were amazed that a male author could have 'got inside the skin' of his female character so convincingly.*

In *Cold Mountain* Charles Frazier also uses his closing acknowledgements to muddy the waters, apologizing 'for the great liberties I have taken with W. P. Inman's life'—so was Inman 'real'? Certainly the American Civil War was, and real wars with fictional people is a popular arrangement: witness *Cold Mountain*, *Birdsong*, *Fugitive Pieces*, and also *Captain Corelli's Mandolin*, where the issue of the writing of history is foregrounded. Dr Iannis struggles with his history of Cephallonia and de Bernières asks us to revisit knee-jerk attitudes to fascism with his charming, mandolin-playing Captain.

Perhaps even more revealing of reading-group taste than the top ten are those authors whose work appeals consistently through a number of titles. Seven of Anne Tyler's books and nine of Margaret Forster's have been read recently by groups. The praise for them offers an insight into what groups value:

— *Anne Tyler's* Breathing Lessons *is well written stylistically so that discussions about style were not a distraction. It is about a domestic situation but in a social setting removed from that of the group so that we could empathize but be objective at the same time.*

— *Margaret Forster—a real favourite with everyone.*

— *Margaret Forster's* Lady's Maid *generated a lot of discussion re historical content and it was enjoyed by all—interest particularly in the excellent day-to-day descriptions of life.*

— *The whole idea (in* Lady's Maid*) of reading about famous lives from the viewpoint of a 'bit player' was intriguing and very revealing.*

Though of course there has to be a dissenting voice or two:

— Lady's Maid *irritated 80 per cent of the group. Tried to turn biography into fiction and didn't convince.*

— Hidden Lives *pretentious and annoying.*

Comments on other successes show what groups want their books to do:

— My Son's Story *by Nadine Gordimer in its style, content, and setting was interesting on many levels. The author chose to write from the point of view of an adolescent boy, highly critical of adult behaviour. The context of the novel was also a rich source of discussion, being set in South Africa and raising questions of racial identity.*

— *We all loved Shena Mackay's* The Orchard on Fire. *We thought it was beautifully written with wonderfully poignant observations of childhood and brilliant period detail. It gave us great insight into child abuse, especially about a child's perception of what adults think and how they are likely to react.*

This power the novel has, the gift of allowing us to see through the eyes of another, is well understood and appreciated. So much so that this could be seen as a central part of the whole experience: the eyes of the other being those of the characters in the book as well as the other readers in the room. This is what the next chapter looks at.

Four

How Groups Talk

'We enjoy feeling totally free to express our own opinions.'

'Discussions can be anything from profound to hilarious, but are always lively.'

When a reading group discussion goes well it can be quite memorable:

— *We had such different reactions to Martin Amis's* Money. *Although this was an evening in 1990 I can still remember (nine years on) how passionately we argued for and against the book.*

Another group has fond memories of its discussion of William Dalrymple's *In Xanadu*, also from nine years previously. What makes for a good discussion? Some groups seem to fire on all cylinders on every occasion, and we were taken to task for asking them to name a book which went well:

— *What does this mean? All the books have produced lively discussions with differing points of view.*

— *All have gone well in the sense that we've had some good discussions, we never all agree.*

— *All books have elicited excellent and lively discussion.*

Others have some interesting thoughts on the matter, and a good range of experiences to draw on.

There's certainly no sure-fire recipe for success or failure, as we can see from the large number of different titles listed as going well and badly. And this is an unstable list, with some authors crossing over and featuring as both hits and misses, sometimes with the same books. Four factors emerged as making for a good discussion:

The books themselves;

The range of opinion in the group;

The background of context or information which people bring to the book;

The congenial atmosphere of the group.

First, the books themselves. Most groups would agree with the comment,

— *We seem to enjoy something which involves a mystery, a conundrum, some ambiguity and its possible interpretations.*

Productive conundrums include:

— *Toni Morrison's* Paradise—*were the characters black or white?*

— *Bernard Schlink's* The Reader—*what would I do?*

— *Margaret Atwood's* Alias Grace: *not only the pleasure of discussing her writing style and characterization, but also the added spice of deciding 'whodunit'.*

— *Ian McEwan's* Enduring Love—*much discussion on the psychology of the book and genuineness or otherwise of the 'scientific' appendix.*

— *A. S. Byatt's* Possession—*very meaty.*

A mixed group of twenty-three years' standing finds that 'nineteenth-century classics always go well'; but on the classics reading groups will have to agree to differ. For some,

— *Rereading the classics always generates good discussion.*

Pride and Prejudice was listed by more than one group as particularly successful, but classics can wilt, even Jane Austen:

— *We all enjoyed* Pride and Prejudice *so it didn't provoke a lot of discussion.*
— *One member loved Austen, one gave up after two pages, and most people thought it OK. Didn't go far.*

Tristram Shandy is a notorious black spot:

— *Try reading it and see what you think!*

Many groups list classics as going badly:

— *Proust's* Swann's Way—*we felt we needed more guidance from those who had studied his work.*
— *Scott's* Heart of Midlothian. *No one liked it except the presenter, who had read it thoroughly. Book too long. Scott is unpopular at present.*
— *Dostoevsky's* Brothers Karamazov—*too long and heavy.*
— *George Eliot's* Felix Holt—*inaccessible.*
— *Balzac's* Eugénie Grandet—*none of us really cared about it.*
— *Trollope's* Last Chronicle of Barset—*turgid and heavy going—but the discussion went very well.*
— *Dickens's* Tale of Two Cities—*flopped a bit.*

— *Dante's* La Vita Nuova—*too neurotic for some—but a hit in another group.*

— *Defoe's* Moll Flanders—*some of the language too archaic. (Those that finished it really enjoyed it.)*

— *Disraeli's* Sybil—*too heavy going.*

— *Cervantes'* Don Quixote—*too long and repetitive.*

— *Anne Brontë's* The Tenant of Wildfell Hall—*verbose.*

— *Henry Fielding's* Tom Jones—*too long.*

— *Stevenson's* Travels with a Donkey—*no one would own up to having suggested it.*

— *Henry James's* The Wings of the Dove—*complicated sentence structure made it a real chore to read—although we all plodded through it, hopefully, but it didn't improve; however, we liked the cover of the book.*

So, a long list, showing that even though classics might not go well in discussion, groups will still pick one every now and again. They can surprise themselves agreeably:

— *We didn't want to read, but then really enjoyed,* Cancer Ward *and Dante's* Purgatory, *which we were all very dubious about.*

— *With Margaret Oliphant's* Miss Marjoribanks *we felt we had discovered an amusing unappreciated minor masterpiece. Everyone enthused.*

— *Daniel Defoe's* Roxana, *a surprise for many of us, especially if (like me) unacquainted with eighteenth-century literature.*

A long-lived American group looks back fondly:
— *Our 'best year' has always been referred to as Our Greek Year in the 60s, when we read the Greek plays.*

Revisiting a classic can work well, as another American group found:

— *Almost everyone had read* Madame Bovary *in the past (years and years ago), possibly as a school assignment, and now brought a very different sensibility to it. It became one of everyone's favourite evenings.*

Likewise for an English group:

— *Our opinions on* Sons and Lovers *were not as before.*

However, many would agree with the observation:

— *I have tended to find that the classics cause us problems, e.g. the* Odyssey *and* Madame Bovary, *not because we have not enjoyed reading them but perhaps because we are overawed by their greatness.*

Part of the trouble with the classics may be, as the comments more than hint, their length. This can damn non-classics too:

— *Edward Rutherfurd's* London: The Novel *was disastrous. Everyone thought it sounded great in the reviews etc. but it was too long, too boring and not very well written . . . in fact only one person read it right to the end (she suffers from insomnia and said it helped her to get to sleep) . . . it nearly finished off the reading group; oh thank God for Captain Corelli!*

Other books which can run aground are those too removed culturally. Sometimes groups deliberately choose books from other countries, but they can turn out to be too alien. *Christ Recrucified* by Nikos Kazantzakis defeated a group who couldn't finish it, disappointing the passionate advocate who had chosen it. Likewise Ben Okri's *The Famished Road*,

— *too far from the experience of any members.*

For an American group,

— *Mishima's* Spring Snow *difficult—meaning lost due to culture and style.*

and for a group in Yellowknife in the north-west of Canada,

— *Naguib Mahfouz's* Children of the Alley *culturally so foreign, a lot of energy was spent, while reading, keeping track of people and things.*

In the UK a rural group couldn't get on with Amy Tan, but were of an age (50 plus) to do well with Angela Huth's *Landgirls*. But since being pushed off base is for some a reason for joining the group in the first place, it may be the new and strange which gets the group going:

— Filth *was something we wouldn't necessarily have read and was provocative.*

— *Eugenie Fraser's* The House on the Dvina *was such an eye-opener into a very unknown part of the world.*

Non-fiction can also fall a bit flat. The read may be enjoyable but the discussion is either too difficult (for example, about *Sophie's World*) or has nowhere to go:

— *J. D. Bauby's* The Diving Bell and the Butterfly— *not much to say after admiring the human spirit.*

Books don't have to be liked to go well.

— *A good discussion on* A Confederacy of Dunces, *which we disliked with passion.*

— *The characters of Joanna Trollope's* A Village Affair *were felt to be stereotypical, the story novelettish, and the background hackneyed. Interestingly though a vigorous discussion was provoked—most highly critical!*

— Under the Tuscan Sun; *lively discussion of what a bad book it was!*

— *The style of writing of Nancy Huston's* The Mark of the Angel *we generally found irritating, so that was food for discussion.*

But some books are thought too lightweight:

— *Books like* The Horse Whisperer, *which aren't substantial mean that we can't get our teeth into discussion.*

And too much agreement can sink a book:

— *When everyone loves a book the discussion peters out early.*

This brings us to the second element vital to good reading-group talk, the range of opinion in the group. The majority of groups identify this as a key ingredient:

— *What makes for a good discussion? That only needs two of the members to really dislike a book and believe me we have no holding back on our discussions.*

— *The group was equally divided in liking/disliking Donna Tartt's* Secret History, *which provoked good discussion. At the end of the meeting some members had changed sides.*

— The God of Small Things *couldn't fail. Three or four members loved it. The others who were less sure began to come round and the 'original' fans saw more and more in it.*

'Heated arguments' are recalled fondly, the hotter the better. Respondents seem to enjoy the fireworks: 'I have to contradict or explode'. Occasionally camps which are totally polarized can fail to make any common cause at all:

— *Elizabeth Knox's* The Vintner's Luck *went badly. Half the group didn't like the fantasy aspect of this novel and couldn't be both-*

ered finishing it. The other half thought it was an amazing book and couldn't understand why the others didn't like it.

— *We were so totally divided in our opinion of* The Divine Secrets of the Ya Ya Sisterhood—*three loved it, three hated it—that we reached a discussion gridlock.*

Other gridlock books were Michael Cunningham's *A Home at the End of the World* and Mary Gaitskill's *Because They Wanted To*, and a session on *Angela's Ashes* which opened up 'quite alarming differences'. But it is the differences which are for most people the joy of the group.

— *What is interesting is that we rarely all agree about the book.*

— *People's thoughts on a book are never predictable, even after fourteen years.*

— *I'm amazed at the variety of opinions about each book.*

— *I enjoy the stimulation of so many different views on one book. Surprising sometimes—given we are all women in the same age group, similar backgrounds, living circumstances, age of children, education, etc. Sociologists would probably regard us all as having similar reading habits and preferences!*

Examples of books for which different responses led to good discussion include:

— Fugitive Pieces: *some loved it, others hated it. It provoked real debate.*

— The English Patient: *some people loved it and others hated it.*

— A Prayer for Owen Meany: *plenty of controversy. Some disliked it, some thought it a masterpiece.*

— *Kureishi's* Intimacy: *feelings ran so high both for and against.*

— *Joe Simpson's* Touching the Void: *some thought him heroic, others selfish.*

Other books which divided responses and provoked good discussion are Golding's *The Spire*, Faulks's *Birdsong*, Mann's *Death in Venice*, Martin Amis's *Time's Arrow*, and Frank McCourt's *Angela's Ashes*. One group finds that 'books that centre on lifestyle seem to generate most argument, e.g. Helen Fielding's *Bridget Jones's Diary* and Lisa Jewell's *Ralph's Party*.' A rural group had its first session with Elizabeth Gaskell's *Cranford*:

— *I was worried that the discussion would not take off, but as soon as the first person had said something, which happened to be fairly contentious, everyone piled in and we were hammer and tongs for an hour and a half. Who would have thought* Cranford *would have aroused such passions? Or triggered off such a broad discussion ranging over political, social, and moral themes? After that I stopped worrying about the likelihood of good discussion.*

The third factor contributing to a good discussion is what people bring to the group. This can be personal knowledge: the group member who had lived in Japan for *Snow Falling on Cedars*, the diary of an ancestor brought in to accompany *Cold Mountain*, or the first-hand experience of a climber to intensify the drama of Joe Simpson's *Touching the Void*. 'Good input from our varied backgrounds' is a recognized bonus, for example a mix of incomers and locals in Powys and Lincolnshire groups. Historical connections can help. *Captain Corelli's Mandolin* and *Birdsong* evoked nostalgia and many personal or family wartime memories:

— *Three members had fathers who served in the First World War and they remembered the effects of the war on their families.*
— A Thousand Acres *by Jane Smiley was very much enjoyed by quite a disparate group of people coming at it from different directions.*

For example, one member is a farmer and appreciated the close, accurate observation of a farming community. Another, who knew King Lear *well, was surprised to find that foreknowledge of the plot intensified rather than diminished its impact.*

The lawyers discussing *Lady Chatterley's Lover* latched on to the censorship issue with knowledgeable contemporary parallels. As groups develop their own histories they enrich their discussions through the comparisons they can make with other books they have read together. Information about author or background can be a useful impetus, especially in the hands of a well-prepared or enthusiastic presenter.

— *Surprisingly,* Titus Andronicus *went well, which people mostly found an unpleasant play, but which produced a very stimulating discussion. This may have been due to the fact that two people had put a great deal of work (a whole afternoon) into examining the work and producing discussion points and queries in advance of the full session. It may be that the secret of success is good preparation put towards producing not answers, but questions!*

— *Usually it's the enthusiasm or prior* preparation *of the leader for the session that tends to determine how well the discussion progresses.*

— *Research is vital.*

— *Most of us were baffled by* Possession*; we needed an expert to guide us.*

— The Unconsoled *was a problem because the chooser hadn't done her homework.*

On the other hand, another group responded to the bafflement of *The Unconsoled*:

— *It was so confusing and strange that it generated some very interesting discussion as we tried to make sense of it.*

The fourth important factor conducive to good discussion seems to be the atmosphere. The non-coercive element is vital for many:

— *It isn't the sort of meeting where you have to avoid getting volunteered for things.*
— *It's an uncompetitive environment.*
— *We do not feel threatened in any way.*
— *It's a safe place, a consistent and welcoming venue.*

This is a place where many friendships have started or continued:

— *Over the ten years there has never been a flaw in the atmosphere of warm friendship and interest in other members' ideas.*
— *Genuine friendships amongst members (who didn't know each other before) have been a substantial bonus.*
— *Often the themes have roused personal or emotional issues and as a consequence we've now become a group of friends, bound by the book group but sharing our experiences.*

The atmosphere of trust is central to the meaning and success of the reading group:

— *A friendly and non-threatening atmosphere; we are careful to maintain a supportive, non-confrontational atmosphere.*
— *A secure environment for raising emotive issues.*
— *We let our hair down and learn to trust each other—it's OK to be 'different' and have different opinions from each other.*
— *We enjoy the lack of criticism of unusual opinions.*
— *It's non-judgemental and non-competitive so there's no fear of ridicule.*

— *The Scent of Dried Roses by Tim Lott went well. It evoked a lot of discussion on several different levels particularly because it struck a very personal chord with a couple of members who felt safe enough within the group to be very open about their responses.*

Groups can get into potentially quite difficult areas. While 'discussion becomes easier as the years go by', that doesn't mean that things are always cosy. A small number of groups were asked to fill out individual as well as collective questionnaires; and two commentaries on the same discussion of Helen Dunmore's *Talking to the Dead* show how differently a discussion can be perceived:

— *The session went well: not because the book had great literary merit but because it raised a lot of interesting issues and therefore initiated excellent discussion.*

— *The session went badly: we quickly abandoned the book for themes of death etc. in our personal lives and when the group moves off the territory of the book into emotional issues at large it can become quite a dangerous place for some members.*

But a level of danger can add spice to an evening: 'I enjoy the chance to reassess opinions; it's challenging'. The value of the discussion to the participants is obvious, sometimes to the extent of therapy—the word appears occasionally on survey returns—but the book can gain too:

— *Hearing different people talk about it brings it alive.*

— *I enjoy hearing the book's story from another angle.*

— *The evening enlarges the book.*

How do groups structure the way they talk, if at all? Patterns vary hugely from 'no structure at all, that's the joy of it', to groups with quite formal rules of procedure. Some revel in anarchy:

— *We enjoy the lack of authority.*

— *Our only structure is someone saying, Well, what did you think?*

— *We have no leader, happy to be acephalous.*

— *No leader, but some are known to be more fearless in kicking off.*

Others keep a handle on the discussion by various means:

— *We always sit round a table to prevent side chats.*

— *First each member speaks for not more than two minutes; we introduced this recently so people gave impressions before being influenced by others, and to give the quieter members of the group a chance to be heard.*

— *We talk around the group uninterrupted while you hold the book. Then open discussion.*

Participation is the guiding principle:

— *Just try and get everyone to join in.*

— *The aim is to hear everyone's point of view and opinion.*

— *We try to make sure we all get a chance to have our say.*

— *The group is respectful of others' views and very little interrupting goes on.*

— *Free for all—all encouraged to speak. No structure other than this.*

Many groups have a leader or presenter for the session, often the person who has chosen the book. Outside the WEA and adult education, groups with paid leaders are very rare in Britain, although we have come across a few, such as the large rural group which meets six times a year and pays its leader £80 for a two-hour session. Perhaps this will be a growth area, much as it is in America. In the UK it tends to happen more on an occasional basis, with speakers and authors, paid or unpaid, sometimes invited to lead the discussion. Library-based groups often rely on the librarian co-ordinating the group:

— *I am the group leader and try to ensure that only one person speaks at a time—not easy!*

The presenter may give a more or less formal introduction—in some cases a twenty-minute talk, but usually shorter. After the presentations, valued for giving 'a new view of the work and often of the member', some groups make a point of going round the room to get initial views and get everyone talking. It may be a 'kickstart' one-word response from each member, and at least four groups give their books marks out of ten:

— Captain Corelli's Mandolin *came top with 8.8.*

— *Everyone gave* Angela's Ashes *10/10.*

A group now in its twelfth year voted for their favourite book after five years and chose Bruce Chatwin's *On the Black Hill*; other groups pick annual winners, their own customized Bookers.

Some groups like to circulate written reviews or questions before the meeting, or discussions may follow a scheme of headings (character, setting, structure, style) prepared by members in advance. One group discusses two books at each meeting—'we try for contrasts'. Or the group may decide that it wants to read aloud:

— *We have evolved a method of choosing relevant passages which are read aloud in the group.*

— *Occasionally we bring something we have enjoyed individually and read extracts in the group.*

An American group had a memorable evening with *Cold Mountain*:

— *We were so taken by both the setting and characters, and spent time reading aloud to each other. (The fact that a fireplace and several bottles of champagne were involved probably helped set a 'mellow' mood.)*

In London a group has been meeting for an hour a week for the last twenty-five years:

— *We take it in turns to read the book aloud (twenty minutes each)—a moment of pure enjoyment in a busy week.*

Reading aloud has a chequered past, not always distinguished. Florence Nightingale loathed being read to, and said it was 'like lying on one's back with one's hands tied, and having liquid poured down one's throat'.[1] But Charles Darwin enjoyed it a lot, especially if the novel contains 'some person whom one can thoroughly love, and if a pretty woman all the better'.[2]

Even groups which seem quite informal turn out to have a few rules:

— *We're strict about the no chat before coffee rule.*

— *No discussion of next month's choice before ten o'clock.*

— *You must have read the book if you want to come to the meeting.*

— *Each person must read the book even if they have read it before.*

— *If you miss the meeting you must send a written critique.*

— *We have a rule where you are not pressurized into reading any book you don't like but you are encouraged to attend the meeting to listen to others' comments.*

— *All come unless there's a real emergency—we're very strict about it.*

Some groups constitute themselves with elected chairs which rotate every one, two, or three years, or with minute-takers or log-keepers:

— *At the end I write down each person's (short) opinion. So I keep a 'log-book' and sometimes add other details: who turned up with a baby, what we argued about.*

Structure is something which may take a while to evolve— 'not gelled yet' reports a new group less than a year old—or move to being more or less controlled as the group prefers.

Long-running all-male groups tend to have the most formal structures. The Decagon has been going since the early 1930s; its founder-members belonged to the same church in north London, professional men who regretted that on leaving college they no longer talked about books. Membership is ten men, hence the name; 'this is the maximum, probably due to the number of seats in a north London living room'. The sons and grandson of one of the founders are members of the present group, and the formal shape of the evening established in the 1930s is still followed. The book list for the year is fixed at an annual restaurant dinner, and the monthly meetings start with the reading of a twenty-minute paper on the text. Discussion is formally inaugurated by an 'opener' who has previously read the paper. The evening I visited— and received the most kindly welcome—the group was reading Dryden's poem 'Absalom and Achitophel'. Discussion was focused, intelligent, expecting to end the evening with a better understanding of the poem, and this is what happened. Classical, biblical, and political references were teased out; the effects of the heroic couplet explored, and historical contexts explained. There's a strict timetable for the evening, and at an agreed point discussion gives way to a mouth-watering spread: thus do wives and sisters minister to the Decagon. The age-range of the group, from the early thirties to 80, and its varied interests, are an unusual and strong point. They feel that the 'formal and ordered' process of the evening makes a good atmosphere for the relaxed exchange of opinions. They read very widely, choosing a mix of genres and periods. Recent choices have included Browning's *The Ring and the Book* and 'loads of nineteenth-century fiction'; the Decagon year starts in September with a long book which members read over the summer.

Our visits to groups showed us how much a discussion can vary in terms of its range and focus. At one end of the scale a group discussing Anthony Powell's *A Question of Upbringing* stuck closely to its text, even to the comparative scrutiny of colon and semi-colon. When it did move from the text, it was to make comparisons with other writers (Proust, Waugh) or to consider the relation between fiction and biography. This was a mixed group, extremely well read, mostly retired, but with ages ranging from 40-something to 80. They offered subtle readings, and the talk was often quite heated but always friendly. For groups sticking close to the text, issues which come up include:

— *Is it good? Is it as good as people have said in reviews? Does it matter? Will it last? Could it have been better?*

— *Ian McEwan's* Enduring Love *started an interesting discussion about the nature of fiction; we try to include some cultural theory.*

At the other end of the scale a group which had chosen two books couldn't get far with either of them since few members had read both books. This was not a problem, since they liked the idea of hearing about books which they might then choose to read. For this group, the book of the month is partly a jumping-off point, a springboard which can take the group in unforeseen directions. The point is that the group chooses the direction, and the book isn't isolated for study as it may be in a university seminar. This is something many groups stress:

— *It's very casual and deliberately not like school.*

— *We're not very intellectual.*

— *There is nothing high-powered, competitive, or pretentious about the group. We are very ordinary everyday working women who enjoy a get-together to chat about books.*

— *We digress.*

Where groups 'digress' to can be anywhere between 'the very personal and the wildly universal'. For some, the personal is what they come for, and they enjoy swapping news of children or lapsing into what one respondent called 'menopausal chat'. Revelations can get intimate:

— Hidden Lives *touched on what families keep secret/don't reveal and this led to some personal disclosures.*

— *Keri Hulme's* Bone People—*a thought-provoking book set in a different culture and raising different moral values. Several members of the group were prompted to reveal experiences of their own.*

— *In our session on* Shadow Baby *a member revealed that she had been abandoned by her au-pair mother, whom she had never met.*

A woman in another group reading *Shadow Baby* had only recently discovered her mother's identity and was too upset by the book to finish it and come to the group; but she didn't want to miss out on the discussion so she sent her husband instead. Others want to leave the personal behind:

— *We have a no-gossip rule.*

— *We never mention domestic circumstances.*

— *Try to keep off children.*

— *Mention of children's activities banned, now extended to grand-children.*

Instead, this last group ponders 'why men of 60 can have beautiful young women falling for them, even when the book is written by a woman'—in this case *Fugitive Pieces*.

The book can become part of a social exchange, with the accent on the neighbourhood network.

— *We exchange news of local events.*

— *Canvas local issues.*

— *We do a bit of fund-raising for local causes.*

— *Act as a mini-focus group.*

References to other books, films, plays, and TV set the book of the month in a firm cultural web. In addition, issues emerge from the books to move on outwards:

— *We use the book as a catalyst to explore other issues.*

— *We start relevant to the text then often range widely. Usually politics, history, or religion.*

— *Spurred by the text: death, marriage, relationships, families, crime, etc.*

Topics and issues listed include:

— *Women's lives (of course!).*

— *Other books, films, Julie Burchill, life, the state of the world.*

— *Religious beliefs via* Sophie's World.

— *Death and people's reactions to it (a Ukrainian member has a different perspective).*

— *Greek heroes via* Captain Corelli's Mandolin.

— *Irish situation then and now and conditions in other parts of the world via* Angela's Ashes.

— *The nature of evil, mothers/children, drugs, nature/nurture, people trapped by circumstance.*

— *The economy, feelings about our fathers, homosexuality (an all-male group).*

'Always varied and surprising' sums up the feeling of many about the issues covered in groups' discussions:

— Ladder of Years *went well perhaps because initially we thought it very low key, a boring woman in a boring environment, but actually we got very involved in discussions about personal responsibility and argued at length about her choices. In the end, we realized, it had been a very deep and stimulating read.*

The remark 'it's interesting to find out how and what people *think* about some important questions' suggests that here is a forum for a level of debate and conversation not easily found elsewhere:

— *The book sparks off wide-ranging discussions of a more stimulating level than (it has to be said) many all-women chats.*

— *Opportunity to discuss issues with other people from other disciplines/walks of life/different experiences.*

A visit to a group which started in Malaysia over twenty years ago and now blooms in the suburbs of London shows well how the reading group can become 'the jewel in the month', as one member described it. This is a group which really gets into its books and into being together; the day I visited the meeting ran from 10.30 a.m. to 2.30 p.m., with nearly two hours of discussion before a 'bread and cheese only' lunch. The book that month was Alain de Botton's *How Proust Can Change Your Life*, and the leader for the occasion (they rotate) came well prepared, with cuttings, academic articles from the internet, Edmund White's biography of Proust, reproductions of pictures referred to by de Botton, and for light relief the Monty Python clip of the Summarize Proust in 15 seconds competition. The previous month the group had read *Swann's Way* and some had been to the film of *Time Regained*. A thorough approach here, and I was also struck by the imaginative use the group made of the book. They read carefully and sometimes critically, but always receptively, with an eye for the gain to be had, which to them seems to be the point of the exercise. They moved in on the question of Proust's relationship with his mother—'Is she the product of his personality as much as he is of hers?'— and finally drew to a halt with the appreciative recognition: 'Amazing how different our lives are from his, a hundred years on, and yet we can all identify with him so strongly.'

Does good discussion take time to build? We wondered if groups change over time in the ways they talk—especially some of the very long-running groups. While one or two felt that they might have got a bit lazy over the years, the majority agreed that discussion had improved.

— *Freer discussion, more relaxed.*

— *More spontaneous as we have got to know each other.*

— *Becoming more open about likes and dislikes.*

— *Less formal but the discussions have improved, everyone feeling less inhibited.*

— *At first we all wanted to talk at once, however, we learnt to restrain ourselves.*

— *Getting noisier.*

— *Got bawdier.*

— *More confident and argumentative over the twenty-four years.*

The confidence pays dividends:

— *The depth of our discussion has grown.*

— *We have become more focused and analytical.*

— *We are becoming more serious but in a relaxed way.*

— *We are more comfortable expressing opinions knowing we have nothing to prove to each other.*

— *We are now more relaxed and ready to say what we think about the books.*

— *Confident enough to challenge ideas we don't agree with.*

Each group finds its own mode of approach:

— *We're getting better at sticking to the topic of the book and are gaining a more analytical approach.*

— *Started off like a first-year seminar at university. Now we all chat away and don't worry about being intellectual.*

— *All structures have been tried and found wanting (over nine years). Lively chaos reigns.*

— *We've started having a second discussion item, e.g. bring your best holiday read, bring a favourite poem.*

— *Confidence grows even after a few months, makes you think more about content and style.*

— *I think we now expect more out of the group and are disappointed if people don't take it seriously.*

There are of course low points, disasters, splits, and spats. A group may take a while to bed in or settle how it likes to work, with one or two injuries along the way; or these may come later as interests or personalities grate:

— *There was a schism, over what I can't remember, but a dogged five of the original nine remained.*

— *We are a splinter group from an earlier group which became obsessed with therapy.*

— *Two of us were told off for not taking notes, so we split off and started a new group with invited friends.*

— *We had a huge split about ten years ago around 'political' issues— the group that split never really re-formed and no longer exists.*

— *We had to disband at one stage for six months as two members did not want to talk about books as much as have a social evening. Then we started up again without letting them know.*

— *One member left after an unfortunately acrimonious conversation with another group member—we tried to sort it out at the time but she didn't reappear—this was upsetting and the repercussions are still around.*

— *A personality clash between two members is beginning to get in the way.*

— *We had two new members who were not able to be integrated. They were aggressive and uncompromising, and two women members felt attacked. We are now back to our happy five members (two men and three women) who have been the core of the group for about fourteen years.*

— *One woman resigned because she is so shy in a group she never loosened up to contribute much—however, she plans to form her own with people she already knows well.*

— *Shaken out 'unsuitable' members so now all very relaxed, can talk easily.*

A few respondents are dissatisfied with the way their group talks:

— *I would prefer more detailed discussions about structure etc, but basically for the majority of the group it's a good excuse for a lunch.*

Some groups were asked individually 'Are there things about the group you wish were different?' US groups were more forthcoming than their reticent UK counterparts, and came out with a range of gripes:

— *One member annoys me most weeks.*

— *Wish we'd try more 'offbeat' novels that aren't in essence 'women's' novels. I'd also like to do some non-fiction such as political philosophy.*

— *I wish we could plan further ahead, and spend less time at meetings deciding what to read next and where to meet.*

— *More substantive discussions beyond 'I liked the book' or 'I didn't'.*

— *Some members never finish the book—it means we can't discuss the ending.*

— *We have never been able to establish a graceful method of accepting new members or at least screening them. Once you screen, rejection is offensive to the member who has introduced the new application. Awkward.*

And a wonderful quartet:

— *Four of the five men wear hearing aids that whistle when they get excited.*

— *One of the members comes with mountains of notes and causes great eye-rolling when his turn to speak comes up . . . without fail.*

— *One woman sleeps most of the way through.*

— *One woman rarely reads the assignment but gives great excuses: for Camus's* The Plague *she read one page only and said she does not like books about rats.*

Back in the UK, one member frankly admitted that the very closeness of the group can be a source of sadness:

— *Julian Barnes's* History of the World in 10$\frac{1}{2}$ Chapters *was a very difficult session for us. One member had read it and wanted to discuss it but unfortunately died before we discussed it, so you can imagine what the rest of us felt like, especially those of us who had been close to her. It was one book I didn't finish and have no wish to.*

It may be the book which makes for a prickly session, sometimes enjoyable, sometimes not:

— *Roddy Doyle's* The Woman Who Walked Into Doors *went well (in a group at a women's centre). Some women objected to the language and it obviously made some women uncomfortable. Other women defended the book as social realism, hence a very controversial evening.*

— *Jane Smiley's* A Thousand Acres *went badly—one of our members was recovering from breast cancer, a subject covered in the book.*

It has to be said that groups can behave badly:

— *We trashed Dodie Smith's* I Capture the Castle *in the beautiful home of a new member and she never came again.*

Very occasionally groups grind into such chronic malfunction that the disbanding dodge is the only cure. But for most people the point of the group *is* the talk, and they talk not in order to coerce each other into a common reading of the text, but rather to enjoy the diversity, the jolt of looking through another's eyes. 'I hadn't seen it that way' is the mark of approval and satisfaction. So groups usually manage to foster difference while avoiding the self-destructive fireworks of Fay Weldon's timely dramatic version: 'Bloody reading group. Can't even decide on a book to read, forget that for a game of bleeding soldiers.'[3]

Publishers are understandably keen to connect with reading groups. 'How can Penguin be most useful to your Reading Group?' asked a Penguin survey conducted in 1999 mainly via library-based groups in the north of England. The UK has recently blossomed with guides, discussion notes, and biographical information, designed with a reading-group audience in mind. The idea comes from America:

Back in 1993, when Doubleday was about to issue *The Robber Bride*, it realised that Atwood's previous novels had been popular with women's reading groups and decided to facilitate discussions by issuing a guide to Atwood's work. . . . Reading guides are issued by marketing and promotion departments, not by their editorial departments.[4]

We asked whether groups used readers' guides or discussion notes, and most said no. Quite a few have experimented:

— *Have used notes, were interesting but it felt a bit like an exam.*

— *We have looked at some publishers' discussion notes but there was little enthusiasm for them. It was felt by some that they were more suitable for student tutorials. They seemed restricted to contemporary novels.*

— *We found the guide for* Birdsong *very useful but others not so accessible.*

— *We use the* YOU *guide and stick to the questions. Very informal, anyone reads the questions, we all answer them.*

— *We have used the* YOU *reading notes but they are not very popular because the teachers among us say that it is like being back at school.*

— *Readers' guides are useful to some extent, but can lead to a formal discussion point by point instead of a spontaneous session.*

While library-based groups sometimes use author profiles or reading diaries prepared by librarians, other groups may be quite resistant to such aids:

— *We are all quite opinionated and find notes too restrictive and O-level-like.*

— *We agreed to avoid any secondary literature.*

— *If we only kept to the* YOU *reading notes, I feel that the fun of expanding our reading menu would be lost.*

Groups don't want to read their books in a vacuum. They provide a rich framework for their discussion through reference to other books, films, and social and political issues, but the point again seems to be that they want to be active rather than passive consumers. The literary context for the book matters to them, but they prefer to find it for themselves:

— *We bring along cuttings, a video of the book if there is one.*

— *We once wrote to an author in the USA and received a reply from him.*

— *I subscribe to* Writers' News *and can often recommend titles.*

— *We often contact publishers for their info. packs.*

Publishers vary in their responses to such requests. Some are understandably too busy to do much, others have opened doors and filing cabinets. In one case the publisher contacted turned out to be the author himself, to the initial embarrassment of the reading group researcher at the other end of the phone. Including the author in the group is an obvious development for authors who can face it, and some groups report memorable meetings.

The internet is more popular than we expected as a source of information:

— *Leader for the evening finds out about the author, often from internet.*

— *We usually read internet reviews after the discussion.*

— *Internet is a good source for more info. on author and book reviews. We have tried Waterstone's guides but sometimes a bit heavy-going.*

I spoke to a reading-group member who had just used the net to winkle out the original letters used by Wallace Stegner for his Pulitzer prize-winning *Angle of Repose*. Would he rather have saved his time by having the research done for him by a reading group guide? Absolutely not, he said; it's the thrill of the chase.

Despite these extraordinary levels of involvement and activity, groups often deplore what they see as their literary shortcomings. They have a sad tendency for joint depreciation:

— *We're not intellectual at all, just ordinary people.*

— *You're welcome to visit, but would find us pretty low-key.*

— *Because we know each other so well after twenty-three years, it's become harder to have a good discussion on the book (it's hard to discipline ourselves to stick to the text).*

Nevertheless they feel that the individuality of their group comes first, something which might be jeopardized by guides or notes:

— *We would rather find our own way through.*

And then again, as many say,

— *We don't want it to feel like studying, it's reading for pleasure.*

Ever noticed the anagrams of writers and FOOD? Keats and Steak... Proust and Sprout... Yeats and Yeast... Charles Dickens and Children's cakes...
Ros Asquith

Five

The Broader Picture

'We have book club in the afternoons as evening driving not safe on the country roads—the kangaroos don't always give us right of way.'

'Food we order in (this is New York!).'

Although most of the replies in our survey have come from British groups, we have heard from many other groups all over the world—too few to generalize from, but enough to colour in much of the world as reading-group territory, and to distinguish some global mutations. Britain's nearest neighbours, the French, do things differently; they learn philosophy at school and meet for discussions at the *cafés philosophiques* which have grown in popularity over the last decade.[1] They do have reading groups too, such as the one run by librarians in the Pas-de-Calais in order to research and publish a good reading guide for adolescents, and in the process enjoy 'échanges conviviaux'. *Cercles de lecture*, or *groupes lecture*, also meet in *médiathèques*. One thirty-year-old group in Tassin-la-Demi-Lune near Lyon 'regroupe une vingtaine de lectrices (eh oui! Où sont les lecteurs? Nous n'en avons vu que deux ou trois, ces dernières années)'.[2]

Men do better in the mixed groups we have heard from in Germany, some of which have been going for more than fifteen years. One group in their mid-fifties grew out of a university class and likes to discuss 'frauen Literatur', which they explain is 'gender literature', mainly written by women. The member of another German group observes that they have 'become more honest with each other' over their eight years together, valuing the 'emotional outbursts which some books stimulate'. A recent success was Ruth Kluger's *Weiter Leben*, 'the best written and most comprehensive account of a Holocaust survivor'. A mixed group in their early thirties say they were motivated by 'the need to get to know good literature in this "jungle of books" on the market'. So far they have read more books by men, 'maybe to avoid any feeling of discrimination with the male members'. Their recommendation of Javier Marias's *A Heart So White* is a reminder that continental European groups read more 'trans-Europeanly' than their British counterparts. We also heard from a Dutch group, keen to clear Amsterdam from the slander which they feel has accrued from Ian McEwan's 1998 novel.

English-speaking reading groups throughout the world mix incomers and nationals to the benefit of both: good practice for non-English speakers and a welcome meeting-point for incomers. We have heard from such groups in Spain, India, and Greece. There are three very long-running groups in Athens (and they tell us of more in the Cyclades), one of them more than twenty-five years old. Poetry is popular because 'some Greek members haven't time to read a long book', and Ted Hughes's *Tales From Ovid* was a hit:

— *Racy narration goes very well read out loud. Greek members had special interest in the myths. Translation very free but gives real spirit of original while adding Hughes's own lively language and imagery.*

Some of these Athenian groups circulate their books round their members:

— *It is a great way to hear about and have access to English-language books (being in Greece that isn't so easy).*

Their methods are similar (and born out of similar needs) to those of the book clubs that proliferated throughout England in the eighteenth century:

— *We start in a circle, each member discussing her reading without interruption until finished. When she's done, we have a limited exchange between those who have read the book, and then go on to the next.*

The commitment and affection come across strongly:

— *Members show enormous enthusiasm for literature, which is their main source of enjoyment and solace.*

The English-speaking world is hospitable to reading groups, with North America, South Africa, Australia, and New Zealand all recognized as fertile reading-group habitats. They are all well ahead of the British game, with reading groups established as permanent features of the cultural landscape. *The Australian's Review of Books* gives 'The Group', defined as the modern 'equivalent of stitch-and-bitch sewing bees', a monthly column full of stylish snacks and pithy put-downs. Book-cafés play host, sometimes to as many as three groups a night in Perth; and book discussion programmes, serviced by

Councils of Adult Education, operate on a large scale, especially along the eastern seaboard of Australia.[3] For remote communities the reading-group network can be a lifeline. Cape Tribulation, for instance, is a tiny community of a few hundred people located in a rain forest three hours north of Cairns in Queensland; a government-sponsored scheme air-drops books in sets of ten, with reading notes, to the group there. Australian groups have also embraced intercontinental variants, for example the South African custom of rotating the job of book selector round the group. Each month one of the members goes to the bookshop with the group's pooled funds and chooses books she likes the look of. At the meeting members pick from her selection and come back with their verdicts and reviews, which guide others' choices. Sometimes by indirection: 'This was an appalling book about under-age sex and drug abuse in the inner city.' 'I'll take it.'

Australians are justly proud of their reading groups, and have generously written to us with detailed accounts. A member of a group in Adelaide describes their beginnings fourteen years ago:

— *As a group of young mothers with small children we were keen to introduce a bit of intellectual rigour into the humdrum world of nappies and teething—and we have stayed together ever since. We are still an exclusively female group, all professional women in our forties—whilst the small children have become university students (and have naturally benefited from having such well-read mothers). Indeed, many of our children regularly raid our book-shelves and ask our advice on what to read next.*

They give us a privileged glimpse into how a successful group works:

— As in any group there always seem to be active members and passive members. Marion and Barbara could generally be classed as pro-active in that they actively canvass reviews in newspapers, subscribe to the Good Book Guide, and are on the mailing list of a number of bookshops in Adelaide. They generally suggest a list of books which have recently been favourably reviewed in a number of different publications. They also take note of winners of prizes such as the Booker Prize, the Orange Prize, and the Pulitzer Prize. Adelaide has a fantastic 'Writers Week' as part of its Festival of Arts every two years and we always try to read writers who will be attending Writers Week and to go and listen to them speak. This adds an extra dimension to our appreciation of both the novels and the authors. David Lodge, Penelope Lively, Nicholas Shakespeare, Barbara Trapido, Alan Hollinghurst, Louis de Bernières, and Arundhati Roy have all delighted us as speakers and readers. Once a list is compiled from favourable reviews, prize-winning authors, and Writers Week guests we have a democratic voting system whereby we choose ten books from a list of usually about thirty by ticking our preferred choices... As we choose our books just prior to Christmas we usually put the titles on our wish list for Christmas and hope to get two or three as presents from family.

A thirty-two-year-old group from 'a very rural area in the Great Southern of Western Australia' still has two of its inaugural members, and four of over twenty-three years. Most are or were farmers' wives and all are professional women. They get their books through a book club library:

— This library is funded by members of the thirty clubs in the area—which covers a semi-circle radius approx. seventy miles from Albany. Each member of each club pays $A15 a year and books are bought that have been suggested by members at the AGM. The library is run by volunteers who keep the catalogue up to *date—each book is entered with a short résumé of story, page nos., etc. etc.*

Another all-women group in Tasmania has just celebrated its thirteenth anniversary:

— *143 books we have read and shared as well as supporting each other through five babies, five marriage break-ups, one wedding, and many house moves.*

Rather more eccentric is the Henry James group in Melbourne. Three friends watched a video of Peter Bogdanovich's *Daisy Miller,*

— *after which we had a passionate discussion, and thought it would be good to make it into a regular event. We then asked others to join us.*

The mixed group of eight are still meeting six years later to discuss Henry James, with an occasional detour to Edith Wharton. The best James so far:

— The Golden Bowl—*because of its complexity and (often delphic) density—it provoked four hours of animated discussion.*

Book groups are also big in New Zealand, where the FWEA Book Discussion Scheme is in its twenty-seventh year, with thousands of affiliated groups. For an annual fee its members are lent sets of books, and are also sent discussion notes and regular newsletters. Here the reading group has also reached the stage: Roger Hall's comedy *The Book Club* was premiered at Auckland's Herald Theatre in October 1999.

North America is currently the reading group's most high-profile patch. Rachel Jacobsohn, president of the Association of Book Group Readers and Leaders, and co-ordinator of online information services for book groups, estimates that there are 500,000 book groups in America today, twice as many as in 1994, with between one and five million members. The boost has come from Oprah's Book Club, but reading groups in America did of course pre-exist Oprah. Their history goes back to the seventeenth century; by the end of the eighteenth century, according to the literary historian Cathy Davidson, informal reading groups were springing up 'in seemingly every county, partly in response to the widespread dicta that education was essential to democracy'.[4] A century later, 'in the very first weeks' of the Hull-House Settlement for immigrant workers founded by Jane Addams in Chicago in 1889,

Miss Starr started a reading party in George Eliot's *Romola*, which was attended by a group of young women who followed the wonderful tale with unflagging interest. The weekly reading was held in our little upstairs dining room, and two members of the club came to dinner each week, not only that they might be received as guests, but that they might help us wash the dishes afterwards and so make the table ready for the stacks of Florentine photographs.

Challenging stuff, but Eliot's Italian Renaissance novel would have had particular appeal:

We were surrounded by a great many Italians in those days when unified Italy was still comparatively new and many of our neighbours had taken part in that great movement for nationalism. In our first Hull-House reading club for foreign-born students we tried to read an English translation of Mazzini's *On the Duties of Man*. It was not always easy reading, although a shared interest that is genuine is the best possible basis for a class. When we had finished reading *On the Duties of Man*, the class with much bilingual oratory presented to Hull-House a bust of Mazzini—perhaps in gratitude that the course was over![5]

At this time many American women seem to have been more communally minded in their attitude to reading than men. Barbara Sicherman's study of the Hamiltons of Fort Wayne, Indiana, shows that while the men of the family were cosily ensconced in their private libraries, 'well-stocked with port and cigars as well as books', the women of the family were busy setting up a Free Reading Room for Women. They were not alone: 'one source estimates that women founded 75 per cent of all American public libraries'.[6] In the twentieth century the Great Books Foundation, dating from 1947, was an important player in launching millions into habits of collective reading, training its leaders in a method called 'shared inquiry', asking but not answering interpretative questions.

The dozen New York society women who inaugurate their Book Class in Louis Auchincloss's novel in 1908, and who meet monthly, 'except of course in the torrid summertime ... until the death of Cornelia Gates sixty-four years later' do well;[7] but many US groups still in existence have been going for over a hundred years. The Setauket Library Club Reading Group, founded in 1896 and still meeting monthly with good attendance, has members who joined in the 1960s. These women take their club seriously. They have a president, vice-president, secretary, and historian, and eschew fiction in favour of well-researched topics.

— *The topic of US presidents and the presidents' wives was very interesting to each one of our members. Many biographies were used, bringing to light facts we never learned in school. We devoted two semesters to these readings which surprised all of us. In most instances the wives were more impressive than the elected presidents. We read updated biographies and hoped the author didn't try to rewrite history . . . . Members may also invite a guest speaker to take her month. When we selected the history of China as our overall topic we invited two grad. students to present a talk. These students had spent five weeks travelling in China. Made our reading of the history, arts, customs, etc. come alive.*

Today North America has the world's most reading-group-friendly book industry. Bookstores routinely offer discounts (you just have to register your group name), and publishers pump out free reading guides and reading-group gazettes, with news of 'Reading Group Bestsellers', 'Classic Club Collectibles', and profiles of contemporary authors. A score of 'how to' manuals bristle with tips and warnings, and one publisher has even brought the group inside the covers. Ballantine's Readers' Circle books include author interviews and a list of twenty 'reading-group questions and topics for discussion'. Readers of Amy Ephron's *A Cup of Tea* (1997) are asked, for instance: 'What do you think of Rosemary's reaction when Philip describes Eleanor as being "astonishingly pretty". Would you have shown so little emotion if it had been your fiancé who seemed to connect with someone like Eleanor?'

The burgeoning groups are clearly meeting a need. A group describing itself to us as 'small-town' answered the question 'how did your group start?' in one word, 'deprivation'. There are, as you might expect, as many reading-group variants as you could wish for: 'If you only want to read Victorian novels, African-American writers, fiction by women, American literature, mysteries, biography, award-winners—it's easy to find a group that suits your taste.'[8] San Francisco bookstores currently offer such specialisms as the Tranquillity and Insight group for Buddhist and spiritual literature, a deaf gay and lesbian group, and a group for devotees of 'great women in French history'.

Some US groups function primarily as circulation networks, such as the seventy-five-year-old Californian group which selects, buys, and reviews books to circulate round its members. A twenty-year-old Texan group owns a big book box into which each member puts a book she thinks others would like, 'and eventually everyone reads most of the books'. Many American book group members we heard from have been in more than one group. The habit can descend matrilinearly—a San Franciscan woman started a group because her mother had been in one for twenty years—or propagate via marriage:

— *In April our male member got married—his wife is starting her own book group.*

Some couples, though, like to read together. A group of six couples who have been reading and dining together for sixteen years find that 'the sex of the author is an important discussion point, and whether the slant is male or female in the book'.

As in the UK, new groups start up because, in the words of a librarian in a Michigan health facility, 'I've always wanted to be in a group like this but couldn't find one to join, so I started one at my work site.' Good collective organization seems to be the key to success for the larger and longer-lived groups. A thirty-four-year-old Texan group, for example, selects its books via 'a committee comprised of those reviewing for the year'; the chair rotates alphabetically and is responsible for putting out a printed schedule of books:

— *Frances Mayes' Under the Tuscan Sun was our best meeting last season. We had a historian give a talk on Tuscany, a member gave a slide showing and review. Our spouses were invited for the annual dinner and we served a Tuscan meal with wine appropriate to the region.*

With *Memoirs of a Geisha*, however, their zeal backfired a little:

— *A Japanese guest was present and she was sensitive about the subject of geishas. We did not want to offend her, so discussion was not as free as usual.*

Energetic US groups distribute newsletters among themselves, with summaries of what was read and eaten, and news of 'local book-related events (e.g. author visits)'. Or perhaps they will try 'pre-discussion sessions'; one, on 'our personal reading histories', worked well. Others like to keep extensive files of reviews and newspaper articles to bring to the group—but read them only after members have given their own opinions. As well as the book of the month, a mixed group of teachers and psychiatric social workers have for the last year all been reading the Harry Potter books:

— *We spend a few minutes each meeting talking informally about some aspect of them.*

And one group has made the leap from reading to writing. The Parachutists of San Francisco have published their autobiographies, so that they can read about themselves: 'As Simone de Beauvoir said, women must become the "subject" of their lives, no longer the "object" of someone else's. We have taken that step.'[9] The step is a logical one, given the truth of Margaret Atwood's observation: 'I suppose you could say that the real, hidden subject of a book group discussion is the book group members themselves.'[10] Many of the groups contributing to Ellen Slezak's *Book Group Book* would agree—'while the books remain our reason for meeting, we have become the story'—whereas I suspect that most UK groups would disagree loudly. This is where British and US groups diverge most. The reading lists which Ellen Slezak has collected from US groups have books on psychology and personal growth which very rarely appear on British lists. And in America reading together and self-help have taken yet another logical step in a healing art which is relatively unknown in the UK. *Read Two Books and Let's Talk Next Week* is the title of a collection of essays by mental health practitioners devoted to 'bibliotherapy... using reading as a tool to assist the therapeutic process'.[11]

In North America, as in Britain, the reading-group movement has been largely woman-led. Not that there aren't mixed or male-only groups, but in the view of a member of a male group, 'While men of earlier generations avoided book clubs because they were viewed as too *feminine*, men of the 90's do the same because contemporary reading groups are seen as too *feminist*.'[12] He is of course right, in that feminism has been a motivating force for some women. Faculty women in a midwestern university started their group twelve years ago (membership now 'FIXED for eternity') from the 'desire to discuss feminist scholarship with faculty peers, to get to know other women on faculty who were roughly the same age and with similar interests' and also because it 'sounded fun'. They read solely non-fiction by women, but while a comparable group of academic women in London plough their way through educational topics, this group's praise for Karen McCarthy Brown's *Mama Lola: A Vodou Priestess in Brooklyn* would strike a chord with many non-academic and not particularly feminist groups:

— *One of the first books we read where author entered into the monograph.*

— *So exotic, lots to discuss.*

— *Roped in all our strengths—one theologian, one art historian, one musician, two foreign language experts with literary interests.*

It is, however, neighbourhood which is, as in Britain, the crucial dynamic—a consideration sometimes taken very literally. The Five Fields Book Club in Massachusetts insists that its twelve-strong membership remains within the fifty-nine households of Five Fields. Snowy evenings make for unpleasant driving and they like to walk to meetings. Friendship is the spur for university-affiliated groups such as Harvard Neighbours, 'an organization whose objective is to make Harvard a friendlier community'. This group particularly appreciated Ron Suskind's *A Hope in the Unseen*:

— *This is the true story of an African American youth from an inner city high school who goes to Brown University. The book relates his experiences for the last two years of high school and first year of university. Because we are a university-based group we all felt very involved in the discussion of this young man's reactions as a freshman at Brown.*

Much further north, in Canada's Northwest Territories, a thriving cluster of groups in Yellowknife shows how the idea can catch on in a community and build both external and internal networks. When a Yellowknife respondent describes the pleasure she gets from her group through 'the realization that others see the same printed words in completely different ways', she shows how the reading group can expand what may seem a small, cut-off community with diversity and possibility.

It may sometimes seem as though everyone—or at least every 40-something woman—in North America is in a reading group, an impression confirmed by an anecdote from Mary Cregan, group leader and author of many reading-group guides:

My friend Laura, who lives on Manhattan's Upper West Side, was recently invited to join a reading group. She walked a few blocks to the brownstone where the group met, and although she remembered the address, she didn't quite remember the apartment number, so she took a guess. Over the intercom she explained that she was there for the reading group, and she was buzzed into the building. She didn't see the friend who had invited her, but the people were friendly and the food was good. It took her about fifteen minutes to realize that this wasn't her group at all, but another one that happened to be meeting at the same time in the same building. What made matters even more confusing was that this group was discussing the next book on her group's list. She stayed for the rest of the discussion and left wondering whether you could go to any apartment building in New York City, explain that you were there for the reading group, and be ushered in.[13]

So are reading groups the fad of the hour, next after jogging and health food? We were certainly surprised by the numbers of relatively young people (of both sexes) in our tiny sample from the US. But on the other hand many groups are very long-lived, and hold a central place in people's lives and affections. A seventeen-year-old Texan group is not alone in

— *preferring to miss their birthday or anniversary dinner than to miss book club.*

Neighbourhood, friendship, and sometimes even more— for a Californian group reading together has had romantic consequences:

— *The big event we are all looking forward to is the wedding of two of our people in October. They had been married to each other for twenty-five years, divorced for fifteen, and are now re-marrying with the book club in attendance.*

But of course every group we hear from, in North America as everywhere else, is stamped with its own individuality: that's what reading groups are all about. Sometimes the name is the clue. The Glitterates in Vancouver City ('Gay + Literate = Glitterate') read mostly gay or lesbian writing, and sometimes pair fiction with biography or related text, for example Michael Cunningham's *The Hours* with Virginia Woolf's *Mrs Dalloway*. A different common interest sent a group of young mothers in New York to read Maurice Sendak's *Where the Wild Things Are* together; one commented,

— *I now read children's books with much greater attention to the artwork, what's left out, sub-text.*

Book lists from US groups suggest a wide range of reading, and one of the reasons for this may be the use of paid leaders. America is the land of book group consultants, advisers, 'enhancinators', and therapists. Mickey Pearlman, one of the gurus of the American book group world, is quite clear about the need for paid leaders and rather brutally points out that there will always be 'an underpaid college professor' somewhere near you.[14] A journalist on the *Arizona Daily Star* reckons that high school teachers may be a better bet than college professors, 'who now tend to concentrate on critical theory rather than literature itself'.[15] Janet Stern is a paid leader who currently runs nineteen book groups in Illinois, the oldest of which has been going for thirty-five years. Stern was originally hired to run a book class in a neighbourhood community centre; her group sizes vary from ten to fifty, with the organization handled by group members. Some meet weekly, some fortnightly, and some monthly. These groups are mainly female and almost all have been in higher education. The age mix is terrific— from late twenties to very late nineties. Group members suggest books they want to read and Stern makes the final selection. She says she tries 'valiantly to stay with the text. Occasionally the discussion will move briefly to a related topic—but *no* personal stories.'

Paid leaders are just one of the many types of professionals involved in the American book club service industry. Bookstores employ book club co-ordinators, counsellors, and advisers. Fifteen years ago Virginia Valentine 'started doing reviews for the very few book clubs' who visited Denver's famous Tattered Cover bookstore; 'now over 400 are in contact with the store, either asking for book talks, requesting information on authors, books, etc., or scheduling meetings at the store'. Her clients are full of praise for her 'excellent help', particularly with book selection (she has three women helping her, and puts out an annotated list each year). Sometimes groups arrange an annual 'review' meeting at the store: 'I told a woman that was working downstairs at the Tattered Cover to be on the outlook for a bunch of old farts looking for our book club meeting last night. She asked me the name of the club and I said, BSD. She said, "I'm not even going to ask what it means".'

Librarians can also find that leading a group comes into their job description. Pamela Lieber has been running a book discussion group at the Merrick Library on Long Island for fourteen years:

— *The group has grown in number so we have two sittings for the same monthly selection, one at night and one in the afternoon. Keeping order is difficult. The participants are very verbal and intelligent. I respect their opinions and thoroughly love to hear what they have to say.*

Group members, 25 per cent of whom are male, range from high school students to retirees:

— *I am proud of the membership—Allen Ginsberg would call us 'the best minds of our generation'.*

Enterprising freelance consultants and facilitators dance attendance on the reading-group market with a seductive array of services. They fix reading lists, organize guest speakers, and lead literary retreats in attractive surroundings. If you live in Denver you can hire Good Books Lately, a book group consultancy devised by Ellen Moore and Kira Stevens:

Instead of simply offering academic-level discussions-to-go, Good Books Lately gives book groups a menu of services to select from...custom study guides in advance of their meetings ($50), study guides with a discussion facilitator ($100), reading lists, and advice on how to get started. (One value add: they come to book group meetings toting a complimentary bottle of wine from Mondo Vino.)[16]

Suzanne Hales of Illinois describes herself as a 'book enhan-cinator'. She may be called in to a group on an occasional basis, 'to help them get more out of challenging books such as *The Bone People* by Keri Hulme or A. S. Byatt's *Possession* . . . or just to have a change of pace or to give their group a shot of adrenaline'. Hales will also arrive in role, sometimes disconcertingly so. A case of dress to depress:

Someone recently confessed to me that when I arrived at book group to do a dramatic review as the character Maggie from Anne Tyler's *Breathing Lessons*, dressed in a polyester dress and a little hat with a veil that I had found at a rummage sale, she thought I must be a new member of the group. She said she felt genuinely sorry for anyone who would dress like that. She was relieved when I was introduced as the book reviewer and discovered I was in costume.[17]

The book club therapist has also arrived. Rachel Jacobsohn finds that she is 'increasingly being called in not just to lead, but to doctor ailing groups; she was recently called in to counsel three "groups in crisis" and spent "hours and hours" on group therapy'.[18]

American reading groups have not operated unnoticed by US commentators and academics. The sociologist Elizabeth Long studied eighty groups in Houston in the 1980s, and came to the conclusion that 'they occupy a social space that calls our received distinction between public and private into question'.[19] Also in the 1980s Janice Radway was research-ing women who read romantic fiction. Although *Reading the Romance: Women, Patriarchy and Popular Literature* (1984) doesn't deal directly with communal reading, since 'the women rarely, if ever, discussed romances with more than one or two individuals', Radway's comments on the meaning of reading in these women's lives can usefully be contrasted with what the groups in our survey say they value. The readers and editors Radway describes in her 1997 book, *A Feeling for Books: The Book-of-the-Month Club, Literary Taste, and Middle-Class Desire*, are closer to the reading-group constituency, and share many of the same preoccupations and preferences.

Reading groups are a live issue in the North American press, where debates rage over their pros and cons. Eileen Daspin writes for the *Wall Street Journal* on 'The Tyranny of the Book Group', reporting 'from the literary trenches' of internecine group warfare: 'Scores of once-genteel groups have degenerated into infighting, one-upmanship and sheer social terror.' Stephanie Nolen takes the same line in 'Why I Won't Join the Book Club': 'The book-group craze is an indication of a subtle, and sad, shift in the way that people are approaching books—as just another status-symbol in their overscheduled lives.'[20] For this journalist, 'reading has become like push-ups', too much of a lifestyle statement, with the death knell sounding for 'organic literary life a few months ago, with the debut of *Book: The Magazine for the Reading Life*. It's a glossy little meal of author profiles and fun features, including lots of tips for getting along at the (of course) book club.' The *San Francisco Chronicle*, on the other hand, launched its own Chronicle Book Club at the end of 1999, complete with discounts, live TV debates, a website for online discussion, and votes for club selections: 'It's our hope that The Chronicle Book Club can help restore some of the joy that only communal reading can bring... starting on Sunday and once a month from here on out, we're all on the same page.'[21] Also enthusiastic was a journalist in

Houston, describing herself as 'overjoyed' when invited to a group on her block. This, she claimed, was the 'missing link', the 'cure for the chronic illness of modern life', the sense of good neighbourhood she had missed in her life since childhood.[22]

It is this need for neighbourhood and the wish to be 'at home' which motivates the flourishing expatriate groups we have heard from. For them the reading group can be a good way of combating 'repotting' stress (plants which are frequently repotted can have problems with their root systems). Shifting populations can make it difficult to keep a group going, but they also make the group all the more important, as a correspondent from Kuala Lumpur comments:

— *Book groups can be a source of great pleasure and comfort to those of us constantly uprooting ourselves and flitting round the world ... Expats come and go with frightening regularity. We try to maintain between four and six members in spite of this ... and choose books specifically about the area we're living in.*

An eight-year-old group in Strasbourg relishes the contact with 'like-minded anglophone women' and usually meets on Tuesdays 'as there is no school in France on Wednesdays'. They owe their existence to one book in particular:

— *One person invited three friends to read A. S. Byatt's* Possession *and to talk about it afterwards over a glass of wine.*

Their worst book to date:

— *Malcolm Lowry's* Under the Volcano. *Dull, dated, slow-moving— oh, so slow ... so we watched the film instead and drank tequila.*

Book supply for groups such as this can be a problem, and internet sellers will be a boon. Brussels also has a ten-year-old anglophone book group, under the auspices of the British and Commonwealth Women's Club of Brussels:

— *We discuss fiction, biography and translations, and because of our membership, Commonwealth writers. Canadian writers have proved to be exceptionally rewarding.*

Diplomats' wives are famed for their reading groups, and often bring back the idea to the home country on retirement. A group of Israeli women in Chicago have been meeting for thirteen years to read Israeli authors in Hebrew: 'the idea behind is to keep up the language and culture'. Discussion ranges widely, but 'never politics'.

'Expatriate groups are a transient society', as a member of a fifteen-year-old group in Singapore observes. A member of a Spanish group which mixes expatriates and nationals reports that 'ex-pat members move on to other countries and hopefully other book groups'. Members of the ten-year-old Women in Abu Dhabi group come from England, Scotland, Eire, USA, Canada, Australia, New Zealand, the Philippines, Syria, Germany, 'and a valiant Japanese lady who really can't cope with the books but tries to keep up with the conversation'. The cross-cultural dividend is unpredictable:

— *Last week we 'did' Emma, the subject matter of which seemed to be a bit nearer to life in Syria than in modern England.*

While their choice of books such as Hilary Mantel's *Eight Months on Ghazza Street* and Paul Scott's *Staying On* reflects their circumstances, they also like to read the 'live' books of the moment that other groups go for too. It's a way of joining in a global conversation, an idea which prompted a Tasmanian group to write to us:

— *We would love to be part of your survey, read about the results and correspond with other groups around the world. Yours enthusiastically.*

Six

The Pleasures of Reading Together

'Reading is no longer a solitary affair.'

'We now see being a member as a permanent feature of our lives.'

We asked the groups in our survey what they most enjoy about their reading groups, and one respondent took us back half a century with her mother's enduring memory of neighbourhood sessions in the north of England in 1948:

— *The novel she specifically remembers is Kathleen Winsor's* Forever Amber *because of its risqué reputation. My grandmother, aunt, and several neighbours 'pooled' their tea rations and brought cakes, scones, etc. to these afternoon readings. My mother is sure that they did not knit or sew whilst she was reading (about two chapters a day, because the book was borrowed from the library). I have not been able to establish why they didn't just*

> *borrow the book individually but it seems that there was a kind of delicious feeling of decadence about this communal reading. It is probably significant that these readings took place in the 'front room/parlour' which was kept for special occasions. She insists that they all did their housework in the mornings so as to leave the afternoons free, suggesting that, even after fifty years, there is still some underlying guilt about this activity!*

Freeing up space in a crowded life is still identified as an asset:

— *A valid excuse for actually sitting down and reading.*

— *We love 'having to read'—so don't feel guilty.*

— *Allows me a legitimate few hours to myself away from the kids.*

Giving your reading a shot in the arm is often mentioned, whether it is the pleasure of the bookshop, the reading, or the group:

— *I enjoy buying books; I now spend £100 a year on books whereas previously I spent almost zero.*

— *I am more patient, I give a book a chance that I might have stopped after about fifty pages.*

— *I have become a Reader. In earlier years I read only what I needed to for my work, and vaguely thought of novels as a frivolous indulgence.*

— *I get more out of the books I've discussed at the reading group and remember them for longer.*

— *We now read more widely.*

— *I read books I never would have chosen for myself.*

— *We're reading books we would never have tackled independently.*

— *Having the outlet for the enthusiasm of a good read. Reading is a private pastime but thought-provoking books lead to discussion.*

It was always a pleasure to find someone to discuss a book with, the group almost guarantees this pleasure.

So it's 'the books, the people', but in an important combination which changes the way people read:

— *You read in a different way with half an eye on the meeting ahead, makes you more thoughtful.*
— *The discipline is valued—reading with a purpose.*
— *Reading in a group is so different from reading on your own.*
— *Often it will send me back to re-read the books with a different viewpoint.*

According to the Israeli novelist Amos Oz, 'The game of reading requires you, the reader, to take an active part, to bring to the field your own life experience and your own innocence, as well as caution and cunning.'[1] This is the game that reading groups relish; they are, as we've seen, a very active readership. And this is not just in terms of buying, reading, and discussing, but also in entering the literary arena. Groups write poetry, publish reviews in the local press, correspond with authors, and invite them to meetings.

— *Most people found plenty of interest to talk about in Marina Warner's* Indigo—*both about the subject matter of the book, where Marina Warner had got her ideas from and how she researched it. We were so taken with the book, one of the group wrote to the publishers and Marina Warner joined one of our later discussions.*

Reading has thus become an interactive pleasure. There's also the sense of achievement:

— *That I actually got off my backside and started it.*

— *I feel I'm learning something new and stretching myself in a way I wasn't before.*

— *I have gained a lot of confidence.*

— *Since starting, three members have gone back to further education and everyone has a positive focus.*

The social contact of the group is the other main gain:

— *Complete strangers have made new friends.*

— *Opportunity for a non-work gathering with work colleagues.*

— *For some members who suffer illness or are widows it is very important entertainment.*

— *Adult time talking about books with sympathetic friends.*

— *Varied people with different experiences of life which they bring to the discussion.*

— *Girls' night out.*

But it's social with a difference. If groups change how people read, they also change how people talk and think:

— *Broadens our horizons.*

— *It's a new vehicle for exchanging ideas.*

— *I am more sensitive to the opinions of others.*

— *A great opportunity to meet with a group of friends and not discuss the perennial issues of schools, children, etc.*

— *I enjoy other people's insights into aspects of the book I haven't picked up. I always leave the discussion wiser than I came in.*

— *We share a common culture which we take for granted but which comes under scrutiny every month.*

Respondents refer appreciatively to the kind of talk which reading groups foster:

— *Stimulating conversation.*

— *An understanding and knowledge of the wider issues will be developed often after reading and discussing the book.*

— *Spirited chat.*

— *Ideas generated by interaction and cross-fertilization.*

— *The fascination of listening to the other members' views and opinions which are often totally unexpected.*

— *Even after fourteen years it is almost impossible to predict the reactions of members of the reading group to a particular book. Even those of us who have been together the longest will say 'I know you'll love this book' or 'It wouldn't be your kind of book, you'll hate it' and will be 100 per cent wrong. So one of the things I enjoy most is the unpredictability of people's responses to books.*

— *Our age differences, eldest nearly 70, youngest 32, gives added dimension to the discussion.*

— *I love the buzz and sharing of opinions and chat.*

— *One of the things I like about a reading group is that it brings together such disparate people whose only common factor is love of reading, and that over a course of meetings they recognize each other's differences, which they have to respect and which can be confronted. I have this theory that the parties in the Irish peace process should form a reading group.*

The social historian Theodore Zeldin has extolled the virtues of conversation:

Conversation is a meeting of minds with different memories and habits. When minds meet, they don't just exchange facts; they transform them, reshape them, draw different implications from them, engage in new trains of thought. Conversation doesn't just reshuffle the cards: it creates new cards. That's the part that interests me. That's where I find the excitement.[2]

Reading groups would agree: this is where they too find and create the excitement. And when Zeldin says, 'now it's time for the New Conversation', they may well reply, 'We're having it'.

Groups also gain from the intimacy and trust which flourish in the congenial atmosphere. Members talk each other not only through books but often, over the years, through some of life's rougher patches.

— *Very supportive group, as there have been several traumatic life events in members' families.*

— *(Over the eighteen years) we have often been able to act as 'support group' whenever one of us has been troubled or depressed; we have learned to trust each other, and this trust has grown out of our shared discussions. And the wide range of experience and networks is invaluable.*

— *We know we can all rely on each other.*

— *There is a very strong sense of loyalty among the members.*

— *Very supportive during my recent spell in hospital.*

A member who lost her sight is kept in her group by a 'noble retired teacher' who reads the books on to tape for her. Members who move away often travel long distances for book club nights, or join in by post—for over ten years in one instance. Groups also keep in touch with ex-members through annual newsletters; this is contact with staying power.

These engaged readers and social networkers sound as though they're living on a different planet from the current batch of literary and social commentators weighed down by 'millennial lamentations'—the phrase comes from Sven Birkerts's *Gutenberg Elegies: The Fate of Reading in an Electronic Age* (1994). The picture that commentators paint is gloomy:

Fewer and fewer people, it seems, have the leisure or the inclination to undertake ... serious reading. ... Joyce, Woolf, Soyinka, not to mention the masters who preceded them, will go unread, and the civilizing energies of their prose will circulate aimlessly between closed covers. The overall situation is bleak and getting bleaker.[3]

Equally doom-laden are the essays in collections such as *Literacy is Not Enough, Essays on the Importance of Reading* (1998) and *A Passion for Books* (1999). With 'the quiet voice of the fading book culture drowned out by ... "media culture"', we are apparently at the end of the reading world.[4] Reports from the social observation post are also negative. The American sociologist Robert D. Putnam regrets the shrinking of what he calls 'social capital' in America. In his analysis, exhaustively documented in *Bowling Alone: The Collapse and Revival of American Community* (2000), people aren't doing things in groups any more, and society is the poorer for it. Reading groups don't run counter to Putnam's diagnosis, because although he acknowledges that they contribute to 'civic engagement and social capital', he can find 'little evidence that they have grown in numbers that would significantly offset the civic decay of the past several decades'.[5]

What are we to make of these gloomy scenarios? On the literary front, complaints about falling literacy levels have been constant since at least the eighteenth century, when the rise of the novel was linked to the decline of everything else: literacy, morality, manners, and obeying your superiors.[6] In the 1930s we have Queenie Leavis bemoaning the dominance of the middlebrow bestseller at the expense of highbrow modernism: 'the book-borrowing public has acquired the reading habit while somehow failing to exercise any critical intelligence about its reading'.[7] While Leavis writes with an intellectual snobbery so confident that even Charlotte Brontë gets a scolding, other readers feel more implicated in the decline of standards. The 1930s memoirist of the Bristol Friendly Reading Society thinks that his Victorian forebears read more deeply, 'with more books about religious and scriptural subjects'. Now, he concludes shamefacedly, 'books of various games such as cricket and golf seem more popular'. This breast-beater seems to be suffering from what we might call the serious grandfather fallacy—the guilty sense that our elders dined higher up the literary food chain than we do. But, as we have seen, reading groups read widely and well, and the literary fiction they favour is in good heart and financial shape, in both the US and the UK.[8] Socially speaking too, reading groups have had more purchase than Putnam's alignment of them with self-help groups would suggest. As Putnam himself points out, women's reading groups provided the 'sinews of the suffrage movement' in late nineteenth-century America.[9] So it seems that the dark clouds do have some sunny breaks in them.

The comments made by the groups in our survey give a good idea of reading-group values and strengths. If we look at the particular books which groups like and dislike, together with the reasons they give, a striking consensus emerges. The premium is on empathy, the core reading-group value. This empathy can go three ways: reader–character, author–character, and between all the readers in the room. First and foremost it's a relationship with character, something often mentioned as a focal point for discussion:

— *which character did we like, hate, empathize with, etc.?*

— *we like to discuss characters—motivations, are they likeable, what could they have done differently?*

The failure of reader–character empathy is what doomed Beryl Bainbridge's *Every Man for Himself*, the title itself so anti-group in its sentiments. It's not difficult to see why Bainbridge's novel met with such disfavour. A novel set on the *Titanic* could be expected to engage the reader in the plight of its fated passengers, but Bainbridge refuses this easy route, picking her cast from those least amenable to sympathy: the rich, frivolous, and often unpleasant. This must be the least promising angle, and I think she pulls it off brilliantly, though reading groups didn't.[10] Engagement is a key consideration for many groups in our survey:

— *We could not identify or sympathize with the characters in Iris Murdoch's novels.*

— *Difficult to relate to the characters in Pamela Jooste's* Dance with a Poor Man's Daughter.

— *Not one character we could empathize with or felt we would want to meet in* The Restraint of Beasts *by Magnus Mills —but we admired the writing in a detached sort of way.*

— *Thomas Mann's* The Magic Mountain *went badly, the style distanced the reader from the characters.*

— *Unable to relate Doris Lessing's* Love Again *to our own experience.*

— *Ted Hughes's* Birthday Letters *went well. We did readings and the discussion was fun; we all sympathized with both people in the situation.*

— *The sympathy the main character of Mick Jackson's* The Underground Man *evoked was unbelievable. The fascination of the slow descent from eccentricity to madness tore us all apart. Obviously this was due to the skill of the author which we appreciated. One member said it had changed her life.*

Bainbridge founders on the second count too, empathy between author and character. One group felt that it was 'as if she got bored or didn't care'. A cardinal sin; the author must care. A book about Belgium went down badly with a group there because

— *the author was contemptuous of the people he was talking about.*

Anne Tyler, on the other hand, gets an accolade:

— *We've just read Anne Tyler's* A Patchwork Planet *and all thought it wonderful. Tried to decide just what makes it so good —it's all so real—you can visualize each scene, the dialogue's superb, the characters live. Above all she cares— Barnaby's life has real value—ordinary people count.*

Margaret Forster is popular with many reading groups because empathy with her characters is high priority for her too. *Hidden Lives: A Family Memoir* (1995) ends with an author's note in which Forster writes of her need to walk the same streets as her mother, grandmother, and aunts, 'until the empathy with them was so strong, and the recollection of my childhood self so sharp, that we all walked together'. Many also warm to her enterprise of spotlighting the maid rather than the mistress, the ordinary men and women who have, as the last great sentence of *Middlemarch* puts it, 'lived faithfully a hidden life, and rest in unvisited tombs'.

Having braced herself to accept an invitation to attend a reading-group meeting, the author Nicci Gerrard discovered that what ensued was not a hostile inquisition but 'A conversation about a book, and a conversation about life. Often it's easier to have a conversation about life when it starts off as one about a book ... this is often how we read: our lives and the life of the book merge.'[11] For reading groups, the relationship between book and world is open; the book is expected to speak about the world, and the world (reading-group observation and experience) is brought to bear upon the book. The point is not to map book and life closely—I sat in on a session where two teachers vetoed the choice of a book about a middle-aged teacher having an affair with a pupil—but that the traffic should be two-way. Or rather three-way, to include the busy internal networks of the group itself. When a member of a group in Greece describes what she enjoys about her group in the words 'we connect', the connections go between group members as well as between group and books, group and wider world. Hence the reading-group preference for realism, and for characters that readers can believe in.[12] And while family and domestic themes play well (Forster, Tyler), groups also like books which take them to different times and places. *Cold Mountain*, *The Shipping News*, and *Memoirs of a Geisha* were all praised for opening doors to unknown worlds. *Wild Swans* was appreciated for 'taking us beyond our experience', *Angela's Ashes* because 'the author made it possible for the reader to enter into his world'. Likewise,

— The God of Small Things *gave a vivid insight into a different culture and way of life. How, with the caste system, some people are always unacceptable. It was quirky, repetitious, sad, and humorous—typical of life, but not our life.*

— Snow Falling on Cedars: *there were so many dimensions introduced. New cultural experience.*

— Mrs Jordan's Profession, Alias Grace, Captain Corelli's Mandolin, *and* Angela's Ashes *all went well; all had interesting settings with which we were unfamiliar, a historical dimension, and unusual relationships between people.*

— *Amanda Foreman's* Georgiana Duchess of Devonshire *and Felicity Kendal's* White Cargo—*women's lives so different from ours.*

— *Rohinton Mistry's* A Fine Balance: *complicated, textured novel which group had to be encouraged to try. Universal story shone through 'exotic' location. A first Indian novel for some.*

Travel writing is also picking up a following, a new and unexpected taste:

— *William Dalrymple's* In Xanadu *went well. This was the first time we had tried some travel writing. We all loved it and have read more by him. Very interesting discussion about that part of the world, personal reminiscences etc. and historical background.*

So reading-group pleasures embrace both what you do know and what you don't.

If group talk is partly the pleasure of shared recognition—'we've all been there', agreed the group talking about Herbert and Pip doing their accounts in *Great Expectations*—it's not about trying to reach a consensus. 'Do we all agree?' was a question which punctuated one discussion I sat in on: its aim was not to pressure members into agreement, but rather to open out and test different possible responses. Another group described how they talk:

— *Often particular scenes/encounters/characters are dissected to see how our perceptions of particular characters/incidents match. This is an interesting exercise.*

It might be said that the reading group is a forum for the kind of talk associated with women: co-operation rather than competition, the model of 'emotional literacy' which values teamwork, listening, and sharing over self-assertion and winning the argument.[13] Reading groups could, then, be seen as part of the feminization of culture, though they are not without their edge: members have to defend and justify themselves, argue their views. If the point is not to reach a consensus, neither is it to tolerate everything, as I have seen in groups I've visited.

In the past, reading groups were sometimes associated with coercion, snobbery, and the closed mind. In 1857 Elizabeth Barrett Browning has Aurora Leigh's strait-laced 'cage-bird' aunt belonging to a 'book-club' which guards her 'from your modern trick | Of shaking dangerous questions from the crease' (*Aurora Leigh*, book I, lines 302–3). Edith Wharton's turn-of-the-century ladies who lunch deal in desperate games of one-upmanship in her short story 'Xingu', and P. G. Wodehouse has a terrific time with Mrs Willoughby Smethhurst's pompous suburban literary society in 'The Clicking of Cuthbert': 'With my feeble powers of narrative, I cannot hope to make clear to you all that Cuthbert Banks endured in the next few weeks. And, even if I could, I doubt if I should do so. It is all very well to excite pity and terror, as Aristotle recommends, but there are limits.' Groups today don't particularly want to be authorities, but nor are they fazed by them. The group reading Alain de Botton's *How Proust Can Change*

Your Life were highly amused by the academic encountered on the net who was keen to dismiss de Botton and fence off Proust criticism for devout Proust scholars only. To them the academic was a comic figure.

Reading groups are about reading in the community rather than the academy. Indeed, being non-academic may be part of their self-definition.[14] Their sort of reading is what French scholars call poaching; groups take over and appropriate their books to read in the ways that best suit them.[15] This is embedded reading, where the book thrives in a live cultural and social environment, and its characters and concerns offer a collective alternative life for the group. Reading in community, and reading for community: 'it has been a anchor in my life', writes a member of an American group for over thirty years. Active and interactive, the readers in our survey are inventive, socially aware and engaged, and enjoying themselves hugely. The reading group is, without a doubt, an institution with a lot going for it: a rich past, a vigorous present, and a phenomenal future.

Seven

The Reading Group in the Twenty-First Century

'Definitely not a flash in the pan.'

This chapter brings the reading group into the twenty-first century. A small follow-up survey conducted at the end of 2001 asked groups what they had read during the year, and whether there had been any developments or changes. Were recently established groups still going, or had the late 1990s seen a temporary fad passing through? And what is their place and standing in the world of books?

The 2001 survey has returns from 130 groups and, as in the earlier survey, the enthusiasm comes across strongly, both for what they have been reading, and for the group itself. To start with the books:

— *A fantastic year's reading.*

— *It is particularly exciting that so many recently published books fill us with enthusiasm.*

Once again, it is the number of different titles read by groups this year which is so striking. Between them, the 130 groups listed 718 different titles, with 528 of them—roughly three-quarters—mentioned only once. They evoke a vast literary landscape, with room for Matt Beaumont (*E*) and Dr Johnson (*A Journey to the Western Islands*), as well as Dinah Craik (*John Halifax, Gentleman*), Andrew Samuels (*Politics on the Couch*), and Pope Brock (*Indiana Gothic*). Fiction predominates, but 160 non-fiction prose titles are listed—that's about a quarter of the total. Fifteen individual poets are listed, as well as poetry anthologies and collections, sometimes compiled by the groups themselves.

All except one of the reading groups' top ten books for 2001 are fiction, new in paperback; prize-winners have done well (Table 18). With seven women writers and three men, the list echoes the trend in the year's best-sellers, with its increasing proportion of women writers. It's no surprise that reading groups, with their high female membership, should provide an appreciative forum for women's writing, though they don't invariably pick contemporary domestic realism. The list favours mystery and magic realism (Harris, Allende, Vickers), and a push towards excavation and revelation. What might it have been like to be the woman in a Vermeer picture (Chevalier's *Girl with a Pearl Earring*), or a missionary's family in the Belgian Congo in 1959 (Kingsolver's *The Poisonwood Bible)*, or a traveller to Tasmania in 1857 (Kneale's *English Passengers*)? Excavation and finding out also get into the plots of Ishiguro's *When We Were Orphans* and Sage's *Bad Blood*.

If the top ten has its soft centres—what one group enjoying *Chocolat* identified as the 'gateau factor' – it also shows that groups will tackle disturbing and challenging books. Most of the top ten met with approval:

— Disgrace *voted the best read. Fierce debate because of our differing emotional responses and our reaction to David Lurie. Powerful book because of the many issues it addressed.*

— The Poisonwood Bible *provoked an animated discussion—opposing views on the advantages of 'progress' and 'civilization' and how negative or positive the interaction of the different worlds could be.*

— When We Were Orphans, *a fine book for a bookclub. Easy to read but deceptively difficult to understand. Lots of opinions and theories about dream sequences and the unreliable narrator.*

— White Teeth, *hilarious, off-the-wall account of race in Britain, a very accomplished first novel.*

Other books which went well confirm that groups don't like to be handed success on a plate.

— *Janet Gleeson's* The Moneymaker, *an unexpected wow.*

— *Rosamond Lehmann's* Dusty Answer, *out of the mainstream.*

— *Walter Mosley,* Always Outnumbered, Always Outgunned. *Suggested by someone's husband, approached with a certain amount of trepidation—'not our sort of thing' and was enjoyed by all and led to a wide-ranging discussion. Its very difference made it appreciated.*

As before, the range of books listed as going well is remarkable, as is the warmth of response:

— Hard Times *was enjoyed by everyone. This was a first; no other book has had such acclaim. It was a good yarn, with excellent characterizations; social conditions wonderfully described and it resulted in discussion of nineteenth-century life and politics.*

— *Danzy Senna's* From Caucasia with Love *hit all the right buttons, from remembering the '60s to contemporary issues of racism and identity.*

— *Andrew Miller's* Ingenious Pain *intrigued everyone. The 'willing suspension of disbelief' required caused lengthy discussion between the GP and scientific member of the group.*

— *John Banville's* The Untouchable *produced a very spirited response. Some of us were old enough to remember the Blunt/Philby scandal and it triggered off a host of memories. Some of us felt the writing was so impressive it was life-changing.*

Timeliness can be a factor:

— *Joseph Conrad's* The Secret Agent *went well, anarchists happened to be in the news.*

— *Jill Paton Walsh's* Knowledge of Angels, *discussed it soon after September 11, lot of issues raised in the book very relevant.*

— The Tortilla Curtain *(T. Coraghessan Boyle), very relevant at the moment in view of asylum-seekers.*

If contemporary fiction is the reading-group book of choice, there are some distinctions to be made. Some prefer books which raise issues or evoke a period. Others take a stand:

— *We have rejected as a group the recent novels wrapped up in historical clothes (e.g.* Girl with a Pearl Earring, Tulip Fever). *Basically because we think the quasi-historical theme disguises weak writing and the history is little more than a backdrop and a marketing gimmick.*

— *We did not like so much* When I Lived in Modern Times *(Linda Grant) and* The Catastrophist *(Ronan Bennett) as we felt that they were journalists who had done lots of research and chose to write it up in the form of a novel. The books worked quite well as sources of information, but less well as novels.*

Some books divided their groups dramatically:

— Bridget Jones's Diary *interestingly caused the most difficulties in a mixed group. We admired the way she could fill in characters within the limitations of a diary style. Only one of our group (aged 40) who had had similar job etc. could really identify. Others of same age found it shallow. Us 'elders' rambled on about the educated woman's post-feminist dilemma!*

— The House Gun *(Nadine Gordimer) brought out very strong reactions, in that the group read it in sympathy with the parents or not. We almost fell out over this book!*

— *Marge Piercy's* Three Women—*great discussion, very heated!*

— *Two people hated the Will Self* (How the Dead Live) *with a passion, 'disgusting, depraved, etc.' while others, myself included, thought it rather original and comical.*

Sometimes the book gets talked round:

— *The J. G. Ballard session (on* Super-Cannes*) went particularly well because initially most members disliked it and couldn't give a damn about the characters. The whole evening was redeemed by one member who had read Ballard's autobiography, so could bring an entirely new light to the characters and events of the book.*

Or it can be the victim of circumstances beyond its control:

— *All thought* Man *and* Boy *mere journalism. Member who proposed it did so because the man in her life recommended it and on the eve of the meeting he told her he was leaving . . . so she didn't come.*

The proportion of   217 male to 169 female novelists (56 per cent to 44 per cent) is about the same as the last survey. Women readers read male writers, but sometimes in a spirit of inquiry.

— *We chose Patrick O'Brian's* Master and Commander *(in the same way we tried a Terry Pratchett) to find out what all the fuss is about. As these books are very popular with men, we tried to analyse why, and why we were all so bored. Our conclusion centred round the use of seemingly important detail and 'facts' which were actually totally unnecessary and meaningless in terms of understanding plot and characterization.*

— *The session on Simon Raven's* The Rich Pay Later, *which was disliked by all, was especially lively, enabling us to use the negativity to identify what the major criteria for a good novel were. We all felt it to be highly misogynistic, reflecting a culture which we could neither identify with nor really respect, with a thinness of characterization, and virtually no attempt to explore the inner world of the protagonists, and that the author had little to say. Would a man in our group have thought likewise?*

— *The three Anthony Powells not v. much liked. Labelled 'a man's' book. Thought to be full of unlikeable characters.*

However, some of the year's most disliked books were by women:

— *Suzanne Cleminshaw's* The Great Ideas: *this year's vote for the one we wish we hadn't bothered with.*

— *Bernice Rubens's* I Dreyfus: *categorically the worst book we have ever read, either in or out of book club. Anachronistic, an unconvincing plot, atrocious characterization, factual inaccuracies; a truly terrible book (but made for one of our best sessions).*

But, in true reading-group fashion, opinions vary. While one group found 'a lot to discuss' in Isabel Allende's *Daughter of Fortune*, another group judged the translation poor and the characters 'unimpressive and light'. Likewise, Melvyn Bragg's

Credo was 'surprisingly well received' by one group; for another it was their 'lead balloon of the year'.

As they settle and grow, groups explore different subjects, genres, and approaches. The emphasis on contemporary fiction can become a straitjacket.

— *Feel we need a change—something different— have been too concentrated in contemporary fiction, but lack confidence to tackle 'the classics' or poetry.*

Some less recent fiction is enjoying a come-back.

— *We get a bit het up about too much explicit sex or violence. That's why Arnold Bennett was so popular* (Clayhanger, The Card, The Old Wives' Tale *): strong story lines, lots of emotion, well written, no explicit sex.*

— Ann Veronica *(H. G. Wells) and* The Yellow Wallpaper *(Charlotte Perkins Gilman) provoked the most interesting discussion, centred around male and female perceptions about what it was like to be a woman without freedom and autonomy.*

— *Mary Shelley's* Frankenstein *was a revelation, so different from our preconceived ideas (from films).*

The short story as a genre is overcoming opposition; groups have done well with anthologies and single-author collections, and are planning to read more. While the bestselling Harry Potter has a relatively low profile, the choice of a wide range of children's authors puts reading groups at the heart of the current renaissance for children's literature (see Appendix for lists of short stories and children's authors read by groups this year). And the general extension of their reading lists is part of the development story emerging from the follow-up survey.

Groups were asked if there had been changes in 2001. There have of course been some failures and tensions, and work-based groups are vulnerable as people move jobs. Moribund or defunct groups may have been understandably reluctant to return their surveys; most groups who responded seemed in good health. The arguments about how to proceed go on:

— *Main issue: does one have to read the book at all, if one doesn't like the choice? Answer, yes, so that you make an informed judgement, broaden your horizon, and judge it in the context of other books read by the group.*

Some say they have found a comfortable status quo.

— *We chunter along happily.*

— *Any changes?—after twenty-seven years we wouldn't dare.*

Others report the need to combat staleness. They maintain momentum by actively moving forward, with book-generated events, and by deliberately varying some elements, be it choice of book or group membership.

— *We've recruited several new members at the same time. This has been very successful and given us 'new life'.*

— *Group now numbers twenty-six so we have split into two groups. Both meet on same night but in different parts of the library.*

— *We are definitely ready for a shot in the arm—we have been up and running for four years now and I feel it is becoming stale. Not sure what the answer is—possibly some males.*

This can work well:

— *After eleven years of women only, we have welcomed a man, who does not seem to be at all intimidated.*

Some men, however, need to learn group etiquette:

— *A few new members have joined this year, males, which has given us more of a gender mix. Sometimes they do dominate a discussion.*

— *The new man is* dreadful. *He thinks we're frivolous, so when we start to talk, he ostentatiously leaves the room, starts writing in a notebook, or begins to open his post.*

But, to be fair, it isn't only men.

— *Last week a very bossy newcomer came. She tried to change the day, the time, the book— not sure if she will come again.*

New ways of choosing may keep a group moving forward:

— *As a result of poor selections we have reviewed what we want from the books we choose, and now instead of the member whose house we are in choosing the book, we are selecting a book for each of the subsequent three months at once by consent, discussion, recommendation from others etc. This is overcoming the problem of a member grabbing a book from a bookshop shelf at the last minute without reason. It was good to have a review of the direction we're going in as it relieved the frustration some of us were feeling.*

— *Rather than a group member selecting the novel which we will read we now choose and order our book for discussion from YOU magazine, so that we all come fresh to the text. We also use the accompanying notes and questions which gives more structure to the discussion.*

Different literary terrain may be a good move:

— *The evening on our most significant book from childhood—lots of discussion. It's good to have something as unplanned as this occasionally. All a big surprise.*

— *Next month we are listening to poems read on tape for the first time. We've tried bringing aloud poems before to read ourselves, unsuccessfully.*

— *We celebrate five years in Feb. 2002, and decided to be a bit 'braver' in terms of content and types of books – more non-fiction, biography, and science fiction.*

— No Logo—*a passionately debated book has persuaded us to read more non-fiction.*

In 2001, some had action thrust upon them, as rural groups disinfected each other's tyres to get to meetings—'a consolation for no hunting during the foot and mouth crisis'. Others have been starting a group in a residential home, setting each other ingenious quizzes, and organizing a book evening for the local Home and Garden Club (in conjunction with Ottakar's).

— *When there are opportunities to extend the experiences set up by the book the evening goes better. We ate sushi with Marian Keyes's* Sushi for Beginners, *and watch videos of the books.*

The book may be the spur to further reading. *When We Were Orphans* led one group to read factual accounts about Shanghai in the 1930s; *The Map of Love* encouraged another group to read more about the Middle East. Or the group may take to writing:

— *Mills and Boon books read to find out why they were so popular. Good fun writing our own potted versions.*

— *As a result of a discussion about differing perceptions of the same book, we ran a short story 'competition' (the only competitive bit was guessing who had written which). A set theme and four set characters produced five completely different stories.*

Authors get a warm welcome, sometimes two or three groups get together for the occasion.

— *Authors who visit groups charge things up.*

— *Danuta Reah's* Only Darkness *went very well, (a) we had the author who lives in Sheffield with us, (b) the novel is set locally in Sheffield, in an area we all know well, (c) the story is a thriller which, while not to everyone's taste, was a good page-turning read. Being able to discuss reading and writing with the author in the flesh made for lively interest and discussion.*

— *In May we invited the author—a first for our group. He got us out of our routines, which was good; he also ruffled some feathers, our discussion spilled out on the pavement afterwards.*

An anniversary or an exhibition can be a useful prompt; in 2001 it was the turn of Chaucer and Blake. The point is to build a bridge into or out of the book. Sometimes the book can extend as far as a trip.

— *Philippa Gregory's* Earthly Joys *inspired us to visit the Museum of Garden History where the Tradescants are buried.*

Groups venturing further afield went to Venice with *Miss Garnet's Angel*, and Delft and Amsterdam with the *Girl with the Pearl Earring*.

— *Ross King's* Brunelleschi's Dome *sparked a book group adventure to Florence in early October, climbing the dome was inspirational.*

What the 2001 survey shows is the active reader in motion. Successful groups have a hands-on approach, both to their reading and to the group itself. They will regularly review what they are doing, and are happy to experiment and make changes if they feel something isn't working well.

How is this readership being catered for? And how are they viewed by those not in them? The media in the UK give generously with one hand, even if they do land a few critical slaps with the other. BBC Radio 4's Bookclub continues to attract writers as distinguished as Doris Lessing and Mario Vargas Llosa. *The Mail on Sunday*'s *YOU* Reading Group is growing year on year, and 'now regularly feature titles as soon as they are published'. *The Times* has an on-line Book Circle, as do leading American newspapers, which in turn get their own reading groups. The Mechanics' Institute Library in San Francisco run a 'Sunday Morning "Salon Style" *New York Times* reading group. Come pore through *The New York Times* and discuss the important issues of the day.'

Library provision in the UK is varied. While some areas are now experienced hands at the game, others are still getting into their stride, and a few groups report teething problems with supply ('book-jams') in new schemes. Many librarians relish this 'return to the reader after the arid IT years', as one of them put it. Choice needs to be tactfully handled. This may not be the place for the well-intentioned promotion:

— *'Pure Fiction' (a list of new fiction by young writers) titles generally a bit dour/bleak—too much of a muchness?*

Bradford Libraries are strong on Readers Days; Essex Libraries host two hundred groups across the county (including 'All At Sea', an all male group 'concentrating on everything naval'), and publish *Booktalk*, a newsletter of events, reviews and group reports. Hampshire Libraries support 'Lads and Dads' groups, and Dorset is piloting an Open Books service with a special membership for all reading groups in the county.[1]

Among the bookshop chains, Ottakar's seem to be particularly congenial. One of their staff members suggested that this may be due to their location in smaller towns rather than large cities, areas with a strong sense of local community, and with customers who see their bookshop as a community resource. The staff at the Truro branch provide wine and special promotions, and they also provide the all-important enthusiasm as keen members of the group. Publishers are also moving on to the front foot. Simon and Schuster, for example, can 'provide proofs, books, and visiting authors for reading groups'.

The biggest change in the last two years has been in the offerings on the internet. Most publishers and bookshop chains now have sites designed to be attractive to reading groups. Groups can also use the net to find out about events, to book holidays and 'Reading Retreats in Rural Italy', to preview books ahead of publication, and to tap into support systems such as the *Church Times* reading group.[2] On its site the *Church Times* recommends a new title every month, and includes notes for discussion. Titles so far include Ivan Mann's *A Double Thirst*, Martin Israel's *Learning to Love*, as well as *Chocolat* and P. D. James's *Death in Holy Orders*.

Practically all the evidence of this 2001 follow-up survey is of growth and pleasure in reading together. But the picture would not be complete without acknowledging that the reading group has its critics. There is condescension and disparagement, accusations are made that 'the reading group killed the novel'.[3] Why?

A group of people reading together has always meant something. Some of these meanings stretch far back into the past. Think, for instance, of the story of the rabbis who argued until dawn in Roman times over the meaning of the

Exodus, or the Apostles carved over the South door of Burgos's thirteenth-century cathedral; they keep their places in their books with their fingers as they lean towards each other in animated discussion. The suggestion here is that shared reading keeps the religious community together, and nurtures the spiritual life. Shared reading also has a place in early secular literature. Chaucer's *Canterbury Tales* and Boccaccio's *Decameron* build in an audience, the characters who listen to the tales. Their shared enjoyment and robust responses—argument, laughter, tears—give the reader a ready-made group to join, and a good idea of what the author thinks reading is all about. In these examples, both secular and spiritual, the meanings of the written texts are arrived at through the collective response. And this shared, active reading stands as a central definition of reading itself.

If Chaucer and Boccaccio evoke the pleasures of collective listening and reading, the image of the solitary reader is much more questionable. Literature has some dire warnings. Frankenstein reads on his own late into the night for years on end; the result is a monster, who in his turn finds education, consolation, and enlightenment by being part of a reading circle at one remove. He listens from the cottage outhouse to the books which the exiled Felix and his family read aloud, 'wonderful narrations [which] inspired me with strange feelings'.[4] And sometimes it is reading together which is the key to creation:

The sisters retained the old habit, which was begun in their aunt's life-time, of putting away their work at nine o'clock, and beginning their study, pacing up and down the sitting room. At this time, they talked over the stories they were engaged upon, and described their plots. Once or twice a week, each read to the others what she had written, and heard what they had to say about it.... the readings were of great and stirring interest to all, taking them out of the gnawing pressure of daily-recurring cares, and setting them in a free place. It was on one of these occasions, that Charlotte determined to make her heroine plain, small and unattractive, in defiance of the accepted canon.[5]

And so was born Jane Eyre. But what seems to have happened is that women, the novel, and collective reading come together to the detriment by association of all three.

The book circle (usually female or female-dominated) comes to stand for all that is philistine, pretentious, undiscerning, and snobbish. Its members are readers who don't like reading, they jump on bandwagons, can't tell the good from the bad, and are mainly interested in throwing their weight around. The last thing that book clubs are about, apparently, is reading. The description of the Hollingford Book Society in *Wives and Daughters* shows Elizabeth Gaskell torn between her appreciation of the lively circle it creates and her disapproval of it for press-ganging literature into the service of class interest:

It was the centre of news and gossip, the club, as it were, of the little town. Everybody who pretended to gentility in the place belonged to it. It was a test of gentility, indeed, rather than of education or a love of literature. No shopkeeper would have thought of offering himself as a member, however great his general intelligence and love of reading; while it boasted upon the list of subscribers most of the county families in the neighbourhood, some of whom subscribed to the Hollingford Book Society as a sort of duty belonging to their station, without often using their privilege of reading the books.[6]

Well into the twentieth century the reading group is open to ridicule from male and female novelists alike. The young heroine in Rosamond Lehmann's *Invitation to the Waltz* looks back affectionately at the meetings of the village Literary Society and its Shakespeare readings: 'Parts assigned, a list of expurgations drawn up beforehand by Lady Spencer to avoid awkwardness, and sent round to each member; so that one's Shakespeare was scored with injunctions to skip, skip, skip.'[7] Thirty years later John Updike's *Couples* satirizes the female desire for self-improvement, in its mockery of Foxy Whitman's middle-aged mother whose ' "book circle has been reading Greek mythology, it seems to be the literary rage this year" '.[8]

It is time, I think, to lay these charges of philistinism to a long-overdue rest. Working men's clubs and literary associations are accorded the respect they deserve: why not the women's clubs? The fact that reading groups are for the most part reading books which will not 'last' does not seem to me particularly important. Ironically, the eighteenth-century women's novels that were thrown away—while the sermons of the period were expensively bound to be left unread on the shelves of the British Library—are now being rescued and repaired at great cost by the Centre for the Study of Early English Women's Writing.[9] What does matter is the independence of groups from the commercial world of book-selling and the inner circle of book reviewing. Their great strength is to be a contrary, stroppy bunch of active readers, certainly not all reading from the same page.

One of the complaints made about reading groups is that they have created the 'reading group book', an undemanding and dreary genre of safe, middlebrow best-sellers created by and for reading groups. The figures from our survey just don't bear this out. If publishers are producing 'book group books', our survey shows that reading groups won't necessarily buy them. The figures for books read by groups in 2001 tell the story (Tables 17 and 18). A book gets into the top thirty if it was read by as few as six of the hundred and thirty groups. Three quarters of the books were read by only one group. The US practice of stacking 'book club reads' high at the front of the book store is only one aspect of the phenomenon. No group would dine exclusively at this table, and some not at all.

— *We lost one member over* The Divine Secrets of the Ya Ya Sisterhood, *she felt she had other things to do with her time than read rubbish.*

Looking at the lists which groups send in, it's the delight in diversity which comes across: the group reading Plato's *Last Days of Socrates* which also reads Ian Fleming's *Casino Royale*. The biggest headache for reading groups—what to read—is one they make for themselves because they resist having books chosen for them. Unwilling to be dictated to, they take a professional curiosity in what other groups like or hate. They do pick prize-winners and books from reviews, but there are no foregone conclusions.

— *Least favourite book: Kate Grenville's* The Idea of Perfection. *Orange Prize winner, confirming yet again that prizewinners are not necessarily good reads.*

— *As you can see, we are guided quite a lot by what books are in the news but this is not necessarily an indication that we agree with judges etc.*

— *We are now not so keen to stick to prizewinning or short-listed awards novels. We feel that many need editing and that possibly the more factual novel is in mode.*

The more the hype, the more the suspicion. Indeed, groups are partly about exercising the right to reply. Hence the prominence of *White Teeth*. Groups didn't want to ignore the miles of coverage, but were on their guard. It came top of the books read by groups in 2001, but it also featured as the disappointment and unfinished book of the year.

— *Difficult going.*

— *Universally hated—very over-hyped, we all felt conned into reading this uninteresting, mediocre book.*

Reading groups breathe at a healthy distance from the professional world of writing and reviewing. They are in a position to comment on 'products of the UEA style of creative writing which can be all too recognizable', or 'skimpy books—obviously reviewed by literati and friends of author'. A sort of self-appointed fifth estate, reading groups enjoy taking on the fourth estate of the media. Their independence is particularly important, given the recent controversy over the practice of publishers paying booksellers to recommend their books and display them prominently.[10] To have this constituency of informed freethinkers, committed to reading yet standing at sceptical arm's length from the business of producing, selling, and reviewing books, is invaluable. They provide responsive audiences for writers; they help to keep mid- and backlists alive; and they can spot and pass on the good word for the one-offs from small publishers or unknown authors. Independent, maverick, unpredictable, and not to be bought off, reading groups are a treasure in the house of literature.

Notes

Preface

1 Lucy Kellaway, 'Novel Gazing', *Spectator*, 15 Apr. 2000.

Chapter one— What is a Reading Group?

1 Alberto Manguel, *A History of Reading* (London, 1996), 117–18.

2 Jacqueline Pearson, *Women's Reading in Britain 1750–1835: A Dangerous Recreation* (Cambridge, 1999), 12.

3 Waterstone's survey of reading habits was devised and distributed by the Reading Partnership. See *Building a Nation of Readers: A Review of the National Year of Reading*, published by the National Literacy Trust on behalf of the Department for Education and Employment (London, 2000).

4 Book Forager can be found on www.branching-out.net/

5 D. T. Max, 'She has created 28 bestsellers in a row', *Guardian*, 4 Jan. 2000.

6 David D. Kirkpatrick, 'Oprah Will Curtail "Book Club" Picks, And Authors Weep', *New York Times*, 6 Apr. 2002.

7 Fanny Burney, *Camilla, or A Picture of Youth* (1796); World's Classics (Oxford, 1983), 400–1.

8 'Reading Group Survey', *Book Marketing Limited, Quarterly Update*, 6 (Winter 1999).

9 For more information, see www.persephonebooks.co.uk

10 For further information about the National Reading Campaign and its ongoing programme, see www.literacytrust. org.uk

11 For details of Readers, contact Tom Palmer, Bradford Central Library, Prince's Way, Bradford BD1 1NN, email tom.palmer @bradford.gov.uk

12 Richard Altick, *The English Common Reader* (Chicago, 1957), 243.

13 Ellen Slezak (ed.), *The Book Group Book: A Thoughtful Guide to Forming and Enjoying a Stimulating Book Discussion Group*, 2nd edn. (Chicago, 1995), 119.

14 Sir John Daniel, vice-chancellor of the Open University, 'What is so special about graduates?', *Independent*, 7 Jan. 1999.

15 Home-based reading groups were promoted in the UK in an organized way as long ago as 1889, with the founding of the National Home Reading Union by Dr J. B. Patton of Nottingham. See Felicity Stimpson, 'Reading Circles', *Publishing History*, forthcoming.

16 They provide the *Concise Scots Dictionary* definition: 'lang whang—a long stretch of rather narrow road, specifically the Lang Whang, the old Edinburgh to Lanark road especially between Balerno and Carnwath'.

17 Mostly We Eat can be found at www.serve.com/tsmith/ bookclub/history.html

18 See Richard Holmes, *Coleridge: Early Visions* (London, 1989), 245 and 96.

19 They are not mentioned in the 1994 *Cultural Trends* report on 'Books, Libraries and Reading', nor their 1998 report entitled 'Publishing and Bookselling in the UK'.

Chapter two—Who Belongs to Reading Groups?

1 Ernest H. Boddy, 'The Dalton Book Club: A Brief History', with an introduction by Keith Manley, *Library History*, 9 (1992), 97–105.

2 Cited in M. J. Swanton, 'A Dividing Book Club of the 1840s: Wadebridge, Cornwall', *Library History*, 9 (1992), 106–21. Female members first appear on the lists of the Sedburgh Book Club, started in 1728, in the 1780s; see K. A. Manley, 'Rural Reading in Northwest England: The Sedburgh Book Club, 1728–1928', *Book History*, 2 (1999), 78–95.

3 See Manley, 'Rural Reading in Northwest England'.

4 'Library Association Survey of Secondary School Library Provision', conducted October 1999 by Sheffield Hallam University; Claire Creaser, 'A Survey of Library Services to Schools and Children in the UK 1998–99', Loughborough University; information provided by Jonathan Douglas at the Library Association, London.

5 Information from Jerry Hurst, Young People's Services Librarian of the London Borough of Southwark.

6 Groups such as this need to use large print and audio books, which need some organization.

7 For information and advice about reading groups for the visually impaired, contact the Reader Advice Manager, National Library for the Blind, Far Cromwell Road, Bredbury, Stockport SK6 2SG, email enquiries@nlbuk.org

8 Enquiries via Olive Fowler at Opening the Book, 181 Carleton Road, Pontefract, West Yorkshire WF8 3NH.

9 Ellen Slezak (ed.), *The Book Group Book: A Thoughtful Guide to Forming and Enjoying a Stimulating Book Discussion Group*, 2nd edn. (Chicago, 1995), 93–107.

10 Margaret Beetham, *A Magazine of her Own? Domesticity and Desire in the Woman's Magazine 1800–1914* (London, 1996), 34.

11 Janet Whitney, *Elizabeth Fry, Quaker Heroine* (London, 1937), 235–6.

Chapter three—How Groups Choose and What They Read

1 Harry Scherman's initial proposal for the Book-of-the-Month Club, which he launched in America in 1926, was that it would select one book a month to send automatically to every subscriber. This was scotched immediately by the novelist Dorothy Canfield Fisher, a member of his first selection committee. She understood the importance of choice to readers, thereby ensuring the success of the club. See Janice Radway, *A Feeling for Books: The Book-of-the-Month Club, Literary Taste, and Middle-Class Desire* (Chapel Hill, NC and London, 1997), 192.

2 For the list of members of the Alliance of Literary Societies, see www.sndc.demon.co.uk

3 Amy Cruse, *The Victorians and their Books* (London, 1935), 202. Ruskin societies and Ruskin reading guilds also expanded rapidly: see Brian Maidment, 'Ruskin, *Fors Clavigera* and Ruskinism, 1870–1900', in Robert Hewison (ed.), *New Approaches to Ruskin* (London, 1981), 207.

4 See Ann Thompson and Sasha Roberts (eds.), *Women Reading Shakespeare 1660–1900* (Manchester, 1997), 3.

5 Olivier Pascal-Moussellard, 'Proust For Ever: Signes du temps', *Telerama* (Paris), 19 July 2000. The Marcel Proust Support Group can be found at www.proust.com/ proustgr.html

6 We excluded replies which came through *YOU* magazine, since their reading is to some extent controlled by what the magazine

is offering. The last replies covered a later period (i.e. after December 1999) and were also excluded from this table.

7 Richard Todd, *Consuming Fictions: The Booker Prize and Fiction in Britain Today* (London,1996), 308.

8 Virginia Woolf, *The Death of the Moth and other Essays* (London, 1942).

9 The *Independent*'s list is led by children's writers: (1) Roald Dahl; (2) J. K. Rowling; (3) Terry Pratchett; (4) Catherine Cookson; (5) Jacqueline Wilson; (6) Maeve Binchy; (7) Jane Austen; (8) Dick Francis; (9) Stephen King; (10) Danielle Steel (*Independent*, 10 Mar. 2000).

10 See Elizabeth Long, 'Reading Groups and the Postmodern Crisis of Cultural Authority', *Critical Studies* (1987), 306–27.

11 Golden's blurring of fact and fiction made front-page news when the 'top geisha' he used for a source threatened to sue for libel and misrepresentation: *Independent*, 29 Mar. 2000.

Chapter four—How Groups Talk

1 Edward Cook, *The Life of Florence Nightingale* (London, 1914), vol. i, 41.

2 Charles Darwin, *Autobiography* (London, 1876), 74.

3 Fay Weldon, *The Reading Group* (London, 1999), 25.

4 Mary Cregan, 'Reading Groups are Bridging Academic and Popular Culture', *Chronicle for Higher Education* (Washington, DC), 19 Dec. 1997.

Chapter five—The Broader Picture

1 See Angela Lambert, 'Letter from Sarlat', *Prospect* (Aug./Sept. 1998).

2 *Telerama* (Paris), 4 Aug. 1999.

3 Linsey Howie of La Trobe University, Victoria, has been researching book groups in Australia; she surveyed a sample of ninety Council of Adult Education groups and interviewed twenty-one book group members.

4 Cathy N. Davidson, *Revolution and the Word: The Rise of the Novel in America* (Oxford and New York, 1986), 65.

5 Jane Addams, *Twenty Years at Hull-House* (New York, 1910), 101.

6 Barbara Sicherman, 'Sense and Sensibility: A Case Study of Women's Reading in Late-Victorian America', in Cathy N. Davidson (ed.), *Reading in America* (Baltimore and London, 1989), 201–3.

7 Louis Auchincloss, *The Book Class* (London, 1985), 4.

8 Mickey Pearlman, *What To Read, The Essential Guide for Reading Group Members and Other Book Lovers* (New York, 1994), 5.

9 Rosemary Patton *et al.* (eds.), *The Subject of Our Lives: Thirteen San Francisco Women Tell their Stories* (Santa Barbara, Calif., 1999), 10.

10 Margaret Atwood, foreword to Ellen Slezak (ed.), *The Book Group Book: A Thoughtful Guide to Forming and Enjoying a Stimulating Book Discussion Group*, 2nd edn. (Chicago, 1995), xi.

11 Janice Maidman and Donna Dimenna (eds.), *Read Two Books and Let's Talk Next Week* (New York, 2000).

12 Slezak, *The Book Group Book*, 209.

13 Mary Cregan, 'Reading Groups are Bridging Academic and Popular Culture', *Chronicle for Higher Education* (Washington, DC), 19 Dec. 1997.

14 Pearlman, *What To Read*, 20.

15 James Reel, 'Rhapsodizing Readers', *Arizona Daily Star*, 20 Nov. 1994.

16 Leslie Petroviski, 'Build a Better Book Group', *Denver Post*, 12 June 2000.
   Good Books Lately can be found at www.goodbookslately.com

17 Slezak, *The Book Group Book*, 166–9.

18 Eileen Daspin, 'The Tyranny of the Book Group', *Wall Street Journal*, 15 Jan. 1999.

19 Elizabeth Long, 'Textual Interpretation as Collective Action', in Jonathan Boyarin (ed.), *The Ethnography of Reading* (Berkeley, Calif., 1993), 180–211; Long, 'Reading Groups and the Post-modern Crisis of Cultural Authority', *Cultural Studies* (1987), 306–27.

20 Stephanie Nolen, 'Why I Won't Join the Book Club', *Globe and Mail*, 21 June 1999.

21 David Kipen, 'Opening Chapter', *San Francisco Chronicle*, 16 Sept. 1999.

22 Gail Rosenblum, 'A New Chapter', *Our Kids* (Houston), May 1999.

Chapter six—The Pleasures of Reading Together

1 Amos Oz, *The Story Begins: Essays in Literature* (London, 2000), 115.

2 Theodore Zeldin, *Conversation: How Talk Can Change Your Life* (London, 1998), 14.

3 Sven Birkerts, *The Gutenberg Elegies: The Fate of Reading in an Electronic Age* (London, 1994), 76, 129.

4 Brian Cox (ed.), *Literacy is Not Enough: Essays on the Import-ance of Reading* (Manchester, 1998); J. Hillis Miller's words are quoted in Dale Salwak (ed.), *A Passion for Books* (Basingstoke, 1999).

5 Robert D. Putnam, *Bowling Alone: The Collapse and Revival of American Community* (New York, 2000), 150.

6 See Jacqueline Pearson, *Women's Reading in Britain 1750–1835: A Dangerous Recreation* (Cambridge, 1999).

7 Q. D. Leavis, *Fiction and the Reading Public* (London, 1932), 7.

8 Radway, *A Feeling for Books: The Book-of-the-Month Club, Literary Taste, and Middle-Class Desire* (Chapel Hill, NC and London, 1997), 90, and Richard Todd, *Consuming Fictions: The Booker Prize and Fiction in Britain Today* (London, 1996).

9 Putnam, *Bowling Alone*, 152.

10 Their disapproval chimes with the rejections which Janice Radway found meted out by Book-of-the-Month Club editors to books 'for their failure to engage the reader's sympathy', see Janice Radway, 'The Book-of-the-Month Club and the General Reader: On the Uses of "Serious" Fiction', *Critical Inquiry* (Spring 1988), 516–38.

11 Nicci Gerrard, 'Readers, I Met You . . .', *Observer*, 2 July 2000.

12 Research in America has also identified this preference in reading groups in Houston in the mid-1980s: see Elizabeth Long, 'Reading Groups and the Postmodern Crisis of Cultural Authority', *Cultural Studies* (1987), 306–27; also in the editors who select Book-of-the-Month Club titles, see Radway, 'The Book-of-the-Month Club and the General Reader', and her *A Feeling For Books*, 280.

13 Deborah Cameron, *Good To Talk? Living and Working in a Communication Culture* (London, 2000), analyses these issues succinctly.

14 Radway finds similar boundaries established by Book-of-the-Month Club editors, for whom 'the general reader was most obviously *not* the academic reader': *A Feeling for Books*, 10. Further, in reports by these editors she 'regularly encounters

a certain hostility towards the academic and the institution-
alized teaching of literature which the editors seem to believe
transforms fascinating books into dry exercises in analysis':
'The Book-of-the-Month Club and the General Reader'. Elizabeth Long, on the other hand, characterizes the mid-1980s
groups in Houston, Texas, as more deferential: 'Most reading
groups accept unquestioningly the systems of classification and
evaluation generated by traditional cultural authorities': 'Reading Groups and the Postmodern Crisis of Cultural Authority',
313.

15 Michel de Certeau quoted by Roger Chartier in *Forms and
Meanings: Texts, Performances and Audiences from Codex to
Computer* (Philadelphia, 1995), 91.

Chapter seven—The Reading Group in the Twenty-First Century

1 For information on Bradford Readers Days email *tom.palmer@
bradford.gov.uk*. For the Essex initiatives see *www.essexcc.
gov.uk/askchris*; for Dorset see *www.dorset-cc.gov.uk*; go via
Community Information to Libraries and Arts.

2 See *www.wayswithwords.co.uk* for festivals, workshops and
holidays; more Italian holidays at *www.montefano.com*. To
preview books see *www.bookmovement.com*. The *Church
Times* website is *www.churchtimes.co.uk*.

3 D. J. Taylor, 'Reading Groups Killed the Novel', *Independent on
Sunday*, 27 May 2001.

4 Mary Shelley, *Frankenstein, or, The Modern Prometheus*
(1818); Oxford English Novels (Oxford, 1969), 119.

5 Elizabeth Gaskell, *The Life of Charlotte Brontë* (1857); Dent
Everyman (London, 1966), 215.

6 Elizabeth Gaskell, *Wives and Daughters* (1866); World's Classics (Oxford, 1987), 521-2.

7 Rosamond Lehmann, *Invitation to the Waltz* (1932); Virago Press (London, 1981), 65.

8 John Updike, *Couples* (London, 1968), 276.

9 This will be based at the Chawton House Library, see www.chawton.org.uk

10 Chris Lewis, 'Cooking the Books', *Spectator*, 20 Oct. 2001; Chris Gray, 'Publishers pay thousands for titles promoted by big retailers', *Independent*, 20 Oct. 2001.

Tables

1. Analysis of the Characteristics of 350 Groups

Questionnaires were completed over the period June 1999–May 2000 by groups in the UK.

The sample size varies between the questions because some groups did not answer all the questions. Percentages do not always add up to 100 due to rounding up and down.

Table 1. *Age of group*

	Less than 2 years (%)	2–5 years (%)	6–10 years (%)	More than 10 years (%)	Sample size
All groups	38	29	12	21	350
Location of group					
Rural	40	26	9	26	121
Urban	33	32	16	19	122
Suburban	40	29	12	19	104

Table 2. *Size of group*

	5 people or less (%)	6–10 people (%)	11–15 people (%)	16 people or more (%)	Sample size
All groups	9	57	27	7	333
Location of group					
Rural	7	51	33	9	113
Urban	11	60	24	5	120
Suburban	9	60	24	7	100
Age of group					
Less than 2 years	11	58	27	4	124
2–5 years	11	62	22	5	99
6–10 years	5	62	33	0	39
More than 10 years	3	46	30	20	69

Table 3. *Location of group*

	Proportion (%)	Sample size
Rural	36	121
Urban	35	122
Suburban	28	104
Total	100	347

Table 4. *Place of meeting*

	Proportion (%)	Sample size
Houses	80	273
Libraries	6	20
Other	14	48
Total	100	341

Table 5. *Frequency of meetings*

	Proportion (%)	Sample size
Less than monthly	27	96
Monthly	69	238
More than monthly	4	14
Ad hoc	1	2
Total	100	350

Table 6. *Age of majority of group members*

	Under 30 (%)	30–39 (%)	40–49 (%)	50+ (%)	Widely varied ages (%)	Sample size
All groups	1	20	33	33	12	343
Location of group						
Rural	0	13	27	45	15	118
Urban	3	25	44	18	10	122
Suburban	1	22	30	39	8	103
Age of group						
Less than 2 years	3	29	31	28	9	130
2–5 years	1	23	34	29	13	102
6–10 years	0	15	33	43	10	40
More than 10 years	0	4	33	46	16	69

Table 7. *Sex of participants*

	All female (%)	All male (%)	Mixed (%)	Sample size
Total survey	69	4	27	347
Excluding Orange sample	66	6	28	228
Age of group				
Less than 2 years	71	2	27	138
2–5 years	69	2	29	99
6–10 years	71	7	22	41
More than 10 years	68	10	22	69
Age of majority of group members				
Under 30	20	0	80	5
30–39	81	1	17	69
40–49	75	2	23	111
50+	64	4	31	112
Widely varied ages	55	13	32	38

Table 8. *Proportion of members with higher education*

	More than half (%)	Less than half (%)	Sample size
All groups	88	12	332
Location of group			
Rural	84	16	114
Urban	91	9	121
Suburban	90	10	97
Proportion of members in paid work			
More than half	93	7	219
Less than half	79	21	105
Age of majority of group members			
Under 30	100	0	4
30–39	93	7	70
40–49	92	8	113
50+	82	18	108
Widely varied ages	81	19	36

Table 9. *Proportion of members in paid work*

	More than half (%)	Less than half (%)	Sample size
All groups	67	33	329
Location of group			
Rural	57	43	113
Urban	77	23	118
Suburban	66	34	98
Proportion of members with higher education			
More than half	71	29	286
Less than half	42	58	38
Age of majority of group members			
Under 30	100	0	4
30–39	88	12	69
40–49	86	14	111
50+	35	65	110
Widely varied ages	66	34	35

2. Analysis of Titles Read by 284 Groups between June and December 1999

Table 10. *The type of books groups read (June–December 1999)*

Category	Proportion (%)
Drama	1
Fiction	82
Non-fiction	14
Poetry	2

Base is number of entries, not number of different titles.

Table 11. *Nationality of authors of listed books (June–December 1999)*

Nationality	Total (%)	Rural groups (%)	Urban groups (%)	Suburban groups (%)
North American	26	24	25	29
British	53	56	51	52
European	7	7	8	6
Irish	6	7	6	5
Other	8	7	9	8

Base is number of entries not number of different titles.

Table 12. *Sex of authors read analysed by sex of group (June–December 1999)*

Sex of group	Proportion of books by male authors (%)	Proportion of books by female authors (%)
Female	53	47
Male	64	36
Mixed	57	43
Total	55	45

Base is number of entries not number of different titles.

Table 13. *Distribution of reading by date of first publication (June–December 1999; all figures percentages)*

Date of first publication	Total number of titles[1]	Total number of entries[2]	Age of majority of group members					Type of group		
			Under 30	30–39	40–49	50+	Wide	Rural	Urban	Suburban
1999	2	1	0	1	1	1	0	1	2	0
1998	8	9	8	12	9	8	6	9	10	7
1997	9	18	21	19	21	16	16	15	18	21
1996	7	11	8	12	12	10	10	11	10	12
Total 1996–9	26	39	38	44	43	34	31	36	40	39
1996–9	26	39	38	44	43	34	31	36	40	39
1990–5	21	25	29	27	25	23	27	25	22	26
1980–9	14	10	0	9	8	13	8	10	9	10
1970–9	5	3	0	2	2	3	4	3	2	3
1960–9	5	3	4	4	3	4	2	3	4	4

1945–59	6	3	0	1	4	4	4	4	3	4
1900–44	12	8	4	6	7	9	8	9	9	7
1800s	10	8	17	5	7	9	13	7	9	6
1700s	1	1	4	1	0	1	1	1	1	0
Earlier	1	1	4	1	0	1	1	1	1	1
Total	100	100	100	100	100	100	100	100	100	100	100

[1] In this column each title has been counted once, so that; for example, Captain Corelli's Mandolin counts as one, even though it was read by eighty-one different groups (Table 16). The base for all columns except 'Total number of titles' is the number of entries, not the number of titles

[2] In this column all books entered in the survey returns are counted, so that Captain Corelli's Mandolin is counted eighty-one times.

Table 14. *Number of times individual titles are listed in survey returns (June–December 1999)*

No. of listings	No. of titles	Proportion (%)
Over 50	4	—
20–50	12	1
10–19	18	2
5–9	66	6
4	42	4
3	59	5
2	77	7
1	882	76
Total	1,160	100

Table 15. *Top fifty authors read by groups (June–December 1999)*

No.	Author	No. of entries	No. of titles
1	Louis de Bernières	83	2
2	Frank McCourt	71	1
3	Ian McEwan	68	6
4	Arundhati Roy	58	1
5	Margaret Atwood	50	6
6	Anne Tyler	45	7

No.	Author	No. of entries	No. of titles
	Beryl Bainbridge	45	5
8	Kate Atkinson	43	2
9	Sebastian Faulks	41	3
	Charles Frazier	41	1
11	Anne Michaels	37	1
12	Margaret Forster	36	9
13	Carol Shields	35	4
14	Arthur Golden	34	1
15	E. Annie Proulx	31	4
16	Toni Morrison	29	6
17	David Guterson	27	2
18	Pat Barker	22	5
	Ted Hughes	22	5
	Iris Murdoch	22	9
	Bernard Schlink	22	1
22	Helen Dunmore	18	4
	Jane Smiley	18	3
24	Jane Austen	17	6
	Peter Carey	17	2
	Jim Crace	17	2
	George Eliot	17	7
	Amy Tan	17	3
29	William Boyd	16	6

Table 15. *continued*

No.	Author	No. of entries	No. of titles
	Bill Bryson	16	4
	Henry James	16	9
	Virginia Woolf	16	5
33	Iain Banks	15	6
34	Graham Greene	14	9
	Peter Hoeg	14	2
	Graham Swift	14	3
37	J. D. Bauby	13	1
	Charles Dickens	13	8
	Thomas Hardy	13	8
	Hilary Mantel	13	7
	Gabriel García Márquez	13	4
	John Steinbeck	13	6
43	Jung Chang	12	1
	Michael Ondaatje	12	2
	Rose Tremain	12	3
	Edith Wharton	12	4
47	A. S. Byatt	11	4
	Wilkie Collins	11	2
	Roddy Doyle	11	3
	Claire Tomalin	11	2

Table 16. *Top thirty books read by groups (June–December 1999)*

No.	Title	Author	Entries
1	*Captain Corelli's Mandolin*	Louis de Bernières	81
2	*Angela's Ashes*	Frank McCourt	71
3	*The God of Small Things*	Arundhati Roy	58
4	*Enduring Love*	Ian McEwan	52
5	*Cold Mountain*	Charles Frazier	41
6	*Fugitive Pieces*	Anne Michaels	37
7	*Alias Grace*	Margaret Atwood	36
8	*Behind the Scenes at the Museum*	Kate Atkinson	35
9	*Memoirs of a Geisha*	Arthur Golden	34
10	*Birdsong*	Sebastian Faulks	31
11	*Every Man for Himself*	Beryl Bainbridge	27
12	*Snow Falling on Cedars*	David Guterson	26
13	*Larry's Party*	Carol Shields	24
14	*The Reader*	Bernard Schlink*	22
15	*Beloved*	Toni Morrison	20
	The Shipping News	E. Annie Proulx	20
17	*Ladder of Years*	Anne Tyler	19
18	*Regeneration*	Pat Barker	18
	A Patchwork Planet	Anne Tyler	18
20	*Quarantine*	Jim Crace	16
21	*A Thousand Acres*	Jane Smiley	15

Table 16. *continued*

No.	Title	Author	Entries
22	*Miss Smilla's Feeling for Snow*	Peter Hoeg*	14
	Birthday Letters	Ted Hughes	14
24	*The Diving Bell and the Butterfly*	J. D. Bauby*	13
	Notes from a Small Country	Bill Bryson	13
26	*Jack Maggs*	Peter Carey	12
	Wild Swans	Jung Chang	12
28	*Master Georgie*	Beryl Bainbridge	11
	Hidden Lives	Margaret Forster	11
	The English Patient	Michael Ondaatje	11

* *English translation.*

3. Follow-up Study of 130 groups in December 2001

Table 17. *Top fifty authors read by groups in 2001*

No.	Author	No. of entries	No. of titles
1	Zadie Smith	42	1
2	Joanne Harris	25	2
3	Barbara Kingsolver	24	3
4	Tracy Chevalier	20	1
5	Kazuo Ishiguro	18	2
	Matthew Kneale	18	1
	Lorna Sage	18	1
8	Margaret Atwood	17	4
9	Salley Vickers	15	1
10	Isabel Allende (trans.)	14	2
11	J. M. Coetzee	13	1
	Anita Shreve	13	3
	Rose Tremain	13	3
14	Melvyn Bragg	11	3
	Michael Frayn	11	2

Table 17. *continued*

No.	Author	No. of entries	No. of titles
	Vikram Seth	11	2
17	Charles Dickens	10	8
	Linda Grant	10	1
	Graham Greene	10	6
	Kate Grenville	10	1
	Deborah Moggach	10	2
	Tony Parsons	10	1
	Philip Roth	10	2
24	Andrea Ashworth	9	1
	David Guterson	9	2
	Penelope Lively	9	5
	Philip Pullman	9	1
	Ahdaf Soueif	9	1
	Anne Tyler	9	6
	Rebecca Wells	9	2
31	Sebastian Faulks	8	4
	E. Annie Proulx	8	3
33	Helen Dunmore	7	3
	Ian McEwan	7	3
	Maggie O'Farrell	7	1
	Anthony Trollope	7	4
37	Kate Atkinson	6	2

No. Author	No. of entries	No. of titles
Pat Barker	6	4
Arnold Bennett	6	3
Malcolm Bradbury	6	2
Margaret Drabble	6	2
E. M. Forster	6	4
Margaret Forster	6	4
Arthur Golden	6	1
Thomas Hardy	6	4
Primo Levi (trans.)	6	4
Rosina Lippi	6	1
Bernhard Schlink (trans.)	6	1
Carol Shields	6	4
Dava Sobel	6	2

Table 18. *Top thirty books read by groups in 2001*

No. Title	Author	Entries
1 *White Teeth*	Zadie Smith	42
2 *Chocolat*	Joanne Harris	22
3 *The Poisonwood Bible*	Barbara Kingsolver	21
4 *Girl with a Pearl Earring*	Tracy Chevalier	20
5 *English Passengers*	Matthew Kneale	18

Table 18. *continued*

No.	Title	Author	Entries
	Bad Blood	Lorna Sage	18
7	*When We Were Orphans*	Kazuo Ishiguro	16
8	*Miss Garnet's Angel*	Salley Vickers	15
9	*Daughter of Fortune*	Isabel Allende (trans.)	13
	Disgrace	J. M. Coetzee	13
11	*The Blind Assassin*	Margaret Atwood	12
12	*Music and Silence*	Rose Tremain	11
13	*Headlong*	Michael Frayn	10
	When I Lived in Modern Times	Linda Grant	10
	The Idea of Perfection	Kate Grenville	10
	Man and Boy	Tony Parsons	10
	An Equal Music	Vikram Seth	10
18	*Tulip Fever*	Deborah Moggach	9
	Northern Lights	Philip Pullman	9
	The Map of Love	Ahdaf Soueif	9
	Once in a House on Fire	Andrea Ashworth	9
22	*The Soldier's Return*	Melvyn Bragg	8
	The Human Stain	Philip Roth	8
	The Divine Secrets of the Ya Ya Sisterhood	Rebecca Wells	8

No.	Title	Author	Entries
25	*Snow Falling on Cedars*	David Guterson	7
	The Pilot's Wife	Anita Shreve	7
	After You'd Gone	Maggie O'Farrell	7
28	*Memoirs of a Geisha*	Arthur Golden	6
	Homestead	Rosina Lippi	6
	The Reader	Bernhard Schlink (trans.)	6

4. Lists of UK Fastselling and Most Popular Books and Authors 1999–2001

UK: *bestselling paperbacks, 1999*

	Title	Genre	Author	Nationality
1	*Tara Road*	Novel	Maeve Binchy	Irish
2	*Harry Potter and the Chamber of Secrets*	Juvenile	J. K. Rowling	British
3	*The Street Lawyer*	Thriller	John Grisham	USA
4	*Point of Origin*	Thriller	Patricia Cornwell	USA
5	*About a Boy*	Novel	Nick Hornby	British
6	*Rainbow Six*	Thriller	Tom Clancy	USA
7	*The Long Road Home*	Romance	Danielle Steel	USA
8	*Mirror Image*	Romance	Danielle Steel	USA
9	*The Eleventh Commandment*	Novel	Jeffrey Archer	British
10	*Who Wants to be a Millionaire?*	Quiz Book	Various	British
11	*The Solace of Sin*	Saga	Catherine Cookson	British
12	*Archangel*	Thriller	Robert Harris	British
13	*Bag of Bones*	Thriller	Stephen King	USA
14	*The Loop*	Novel	Nicholas Evans	British

	Title	Genre	Author	Nationality
15	*The Klone and I*	Romance	Danielle Steel	USA
16	*Tell Me Your Dreams*	Thriller	Sidney Sheldon	USA
17	*Charlotte Gray*	Novel	Sebastian Faulks	British
18	*When the Wind Blows*	Thriller	James Patterson	USA
19	*Field of 13*	Crime	Dick Francis	British
20	*Carpe Jugulum*	Fantasy	Terry Pratchett	British
21	*Riley*	Saga	Catherine Cookson	British
22	*Notes from a Big Country*	Travel	Bill Bryson	USA
23	*Southern Cross*	Thriller	Patricia Cornwell	USA
24	*Other People's Children*	Novel	Joanna Trollope	British
25	*The Last Continent*	Fantasy	Terry Pratchett	British
26	*The Breaker*	Crime	Minette Walters	British
27	*The Gilded Cage*	Saga	Josephine Cox	British
28	*A Widow for One Year*	Novel	John Irving	USA
29	*Tomorrow the World*	Saga	Josephine Cox	British
30	*A Sight for Sore Eyes*	Thriller	Ruth Rendell	British

Source: Guardian, 8 Jan. 2000, compiled by Alex Hamilton.

The top thirty writers, UK, 1999

1	Bill Bryson	16	Thomas Hardy
2	Ian McEwan	17	Ruth Rendell
3	Maeve Binchy	18	Jane Austen
4	Louis de Bernières	19	Margaret Forster
5	Sebastian Faulks	20	Stephen King
6	Terry Pratchett	21	Frank McCourt
7	Anne Tyler	22	Toni Morrison
8	Patricia Cornwell	23	Iris Murdoch
9	Charles Dickens	24	Minette Walters
10	Bernard Cornwell	25	Margaret Atwood
11	John Grisham	26	Paul Auster
12	Ian Rankin	27	Bruce Chatwin
13	Charles Frazier	28	Robert Goddard
14	Nick Hornby	29	William Shakespeare
15	Ted Hughes	30	Jeffrey Archer

Source: Waterstone's Reading Survey/AMS.

UK: *fastselling paperbacks,* 2000

Title	Genre	Author	Nationality
1 *The Testament*	Thriller	John Grisham	USA
2 *Hannibal*	Thriller	Thomas Harris	USA
3 *Bridget Jones: The Edge of Reason*	City Girl	Helen Fielding	British
4 *'Tis*	Autobiography	Frank McCourt	USA
5 *The Prisoner of Azkaban*	Juvenile	J. K. Rowling	British
6 *Monsoon*	Adventure	Wilbur Smith	South Africa
7 *Black Notice*	Thriller	Patricia Cornwell	USA
8 *Man and Boy*	Novel	Tony Parsons	British
9 *Score!*	Saga	Jilly Cooper	British
10 *Adrian Mole: The Cappuccino Years*	Novel	Sue Townsend	British
11 *Bittersweet*	Romance	Danielle Steel	USA
12 *Almost A Crime*	Saga	Penny Vincenzi	British
13 *Granny Dan*	Romance	Danielle Steel	USA
14 *Second Wind*	Thriller	Dick Francis	British
15 *Last Chance Saloon*	City Girl	Marian Keyes	Ireland
16 *Irresistible Forces*	Romance	Danielle Steel	USA
17 *The Blind Years*	Saga	Catherine Cookson	British
18 *Pop Goes the Weasel*	Thriller	James Patterson	USA
19 *Inconceivable*	Novel	Ben Elton	British
20 *The Fifth Elephant*	Novel	Terry Pratchett	British
21 *Somewhere, Someday*	Saga	Josephine Cox	British

UK: fastselling paperbacks, 2000 (continued)

	Title	Genre	Author	Nationality
22	Timeline	Thriller	Michael Crichton	USA
23	A House Divided	Saga	Catherine Cookson	British
24	Chocolat	Novel	Joanne Harris	British
25	The Thursday Friend	Saga	Catherine Cookson	British
26	Hearts in Atlantis	Novel	Stephen King	USA
27	The Remorseful Day	Crime	Colin Dexter	British
28	Crisis Four	Thriller	Andy McNab	British
29	Millionaire Ultimate Challenge	Quizbook	Celador	British
30	Rainbow Days	Saga	Josephine Cox	British

Source: The Bookseller, 5 Jan. 2001, compiled by Alex Hamilton

UK: *fastselling paperbacks, 2001*

	Title	Genre	Author	Nationality
1	*Harry Potter and the Goblet of Fire*	Juvenile	J. K. Rowling	British
2	*The Brethren*	Thriller	John Grisham	USA
3	*Scarlet Feather*	Novel	Maeve Binchy	Ireland
4	*A Child Called 'It'*	Autobiography	Dave Pelzer	USA
5	*White Teeth*	Novel	Zadie Smith	British
6	*The Last Precinct*	Crime	Patricia Cornwell	USA
7	*Sushi for Beginners*	Chick lit	Marian Keyes	Ireland
8	*Marrying the Mistress*	Novel	Joanna Trollope	British
9	*The Lost Boy*	Autobiography	Dave Pelzer	USA
10	*The Falls*	Thriller	Ian Rankin	British
11	*Down Under*	Travel	Bill Bryson	USA
12	*The Bear and the Dragon*	Thriller	Tom Clancy	USA
13	*The Blind Assassin*	Novel	Margaret Atwood	Canada
14	*Winter Solstice*	Novel	Rosamunde Pilcher	British
15	*The Sky is Falling*	Thriller	Sidney Sheldon	USA
16	*No Angel*	Saga	Penny Vincenzi	British
17	*McCarthy's Bar*	Travel	Pete McCarthy	British
18	*Blackberry Wine*	Novel	Joanne Harris	British
19	*The Wedding*	Novel	Danielle Steel	USA
20	*Eden: The Guide*	Guide	Various	British
21	*Kate Hannigan's Girl*	Novel	Catherine Cookson	British

UK: fastselling paperbacks, 2001 (continued)

Title	Genre	Author	Nationality
22 *Shattered*	Thriller	Dick Francis	British
23 *Roses are Red*	Thriller	James Patterson	USA
24 *When We Were Orphans*	Novel	Kazuo Ishiguro	British
25 *Cradle and All*	Thriller	James Patterson	USA
26 *A Darkness More than Night*	Thriller	Michael Connelly	USA
27 *The House on Hope Street*	Novel	Danielle Steel	USA
28 *The Shape of Snakes*	Crime	Minette Walters	British
29 *Journey*	Novel	Danielle Steel	USA
30 *The Truth*	Fantasy	Terry Pratchett	British

Source: *Guardian*, 29 December 2001, compiled by Alex Hamilton.

Appendix: Listings

Publications and Guides, updated for 2002–2003 Edition

Publishers' reading guides can best be found via the publisher's site on the internet. Your local public library will provide free access to the internet, you may need to book in advance.

BBC Bookclub Booklet, *How To Run a Book Club*, £2.99 inclusive of postage and packing, payable to BBC Education Production, Bookclub, PO Box 20, Tonbridge, TN12 6WU.

'The Book Lover's Guide to the Internet', compiled by Bradford Libraries, available from the Central Library, Prince's Way, Bradford, West Yorkshire BD1 1NN, or www.reader2reader.com or email: tom.palmer@bradford.gov.uk

Book, The Magazine for the Reading Life, bi-monthly American magazine with features and reviews, see www.bookmagazine.com

Books and Company, quarterly journal edited by Susan Hill. Books and Company, Ebrington, Gloucestershire, GL55 6NW, tel 01386 593 443, email: sales@booksandcompany.co.uk

The Good Book Guide, bi-monthly magazine offering discounts and a wealth of short informative reviews. 61 Frith Street, London W1D 3GB, tel. 020 7490 0900, email: enquiries@gbgdirect.com

Jacobsohn, Rachel W. , *The Reading Group Handbook: Everything You Need To Know To Start Your Own Book Club* (New York: Hyperion, 1998).

McLeish, Kenneth, *Bloomsbury Good Reading Guide* (London: Bloomsbury, 1996).

newBOOKS.mag, UK magazine for readers and reading groups, from bookshops and libraries; free introductory copy from 15 Scots Drive, Wokingham, RG41 3XF, email: guypringle@waitrose.com

Oxford World's Classics Magazine has a regular slot for reading groups, available from the Direct Marketing Team, Trade and Reference Department, Oxford University Press, FREEPOST (SCE10539), Oxford, OX2 6YN, email: worlds.classics@oup.co.uk

Pearlman, Mickey, *What To Read: The Essential Guide for Reading Group Members and Other Book Lovers* (New York: Harper-Collins, 1994).

The Reader, 'A magazine about writing worth reading', two issues a year. *The Reader*, English Department, University of Liverpool, Liverpool L69 7ZR, email: readers@thereader.co.uk

Reading Groups Newsletter, with details of Vintage and Arrow Reading Guides, from Reading Guides, Marketing Dept, Random House, 20 Vauxhall Bridge Road, London SW1V 2SA, tel. 020 7840 8635, email: readingguides@randomhouse.co.uk.

Rogers, Jane (ed.), *Good Fiction Guide* (Oxford: Oxford University Press, 2001), subject essays and more than 1,000 entries on individual writers.

Slezak, Ellen (ed.), *The Book Group Book, A Thoughtful Guide to Forming and Enjoying a Stimulating Book Discussion Group* (Chicago: Chicago Review Press, 1995).

The Toolbox, described as 'A box of delight for readers': orders via Reading Group Toolbox Co-ordinator, Waterstone's CLS, 14 Brewery Road, King's Cross, London N7 9NH, tel. 020 7619 7500, or from local library authorities in England.

Waterstone's Books Quarterly, articles, reviews, and interviews, from all branches of Waterstone's.

Websites

Most publishers and bookshop chains have websites designed to attract and help reading groups, with pages of literary news, reviews, author interviews, and reading guides. Listed below are some less obvious sites. You might also like to try entering 'reading groups' into your search engine, to see what comes up.

www.alphabetstreet.infront.co.uk/
'First chapters' section has author interviews, biographies, book news, and reviews.

www.bbc.co.uk/arts/books/club
News of Radio 4's Bookclub choices and comments from listeners, plus events and courses of interest, and a section on how to set up and run a book club.

www.bol.com
Special features include 'First Fiction—the latest fresh new talent' and 'the 100 Greatest Books—how many have you read?'

www.bookbrowser.com
An American site with reviews, author information and interviews, reading lists, and well updated links to a legion of online book discussions.

www.bookgroup.info
Recommendations, news and 'Book group of the month' feature from a ten year old UK group.

www.bookmuse.com
'Book Discussions Made Smarter', young American site with tips and suggestions. 'We aim for a "voice" on the site that is literary in a

lively, friendly way and that invites our readers' interaction with us and with each other.'

www.booktrust.org.uk
UK charity 'bringing books and people together'. Information, links to other book organizations, and see 'Bookmates, promoting and supporting reading groups'.

www.branching-out.net/
Many possibilities for reading groups: suggestions for reading including the Book Forager facility, 'an easy way to find the kind of read you are looking for'. Branching Out is an initiative from the Society of Chief Librarians.

www.britishcouncil.org/arts/literature
News of publications, events, exhibitions, and a complete listing of UK literature festivals.

www.greatbooks.org
The Great Books Foundation was started by Mortimer Adler in the US in 1947. Adler died in 2001, he was still leading groups in his late 90s.

www.his.com/~allegria/compend.html
Rachel Jacobsohn's site, with Rachel's Compendium of Online Book Discussions.

www.literacytrust.org.uk
Literacy aspects and initiatives, research into reading habits.

www.openingthebook.com
Opening the Book is a consultancy which 'creates resources for readers'; site has links and suggestions for reading.

www.oprah.com
For Oprah Winfrey's Book Club and O, The Oprah Magazine. Features include 'Browse Famous Bookshelves'.

www.oup.co.uk/ or www.worldsclassics.co.uk.
The World's Classics Magazine has a regular slot for reading groups.

www.reader2reader.com
Site for Bradford Libraries, experts and innovators in library reading groups. Helpful site, includes 'The Book Lover's Guide to the Internet'.

www.readinggroupsonline.com.
The site for AOL. Click on Book Clique Café. 'Our Reading Community' has been supporting active readers "online" since 1996'.

www.thegoodbookguide.com/gbg/reading_groups.asp
'If you are a member of a group or would like to start one, this is the page for you.' Discussion boards, recommendations, a Virtual Reading Group, and excellent links for e.g. publishers' reading guides.

www.thereader.co.uk
Site for *The Reader* magazine, 'aimed at the intelligent but non-specialist reader'.

www.trace.ntu.ac.uk
Run by Nottingham Trent University, 'connects writers and readers around the world in real and virtual space'.

www.whatamigoingtoread.com
Discussion is the strength here; you can find out about future discussions, which gives you time to read the book.

www.worldbookday.com
Events and activities for World Book Day in March.

www.you-reading-group.co.uk
Site for the *Mail on Sunday*'s *YOU* reading group.

Reading Lists from Reading Groups 1990–2001

We invited groups to send us their reading lists and records, and over seventy groups did, some with lists going back many years. We are very grateful to them for sharing them with us, and have chosen nine. There are also eleven lists for 2000–1, with a variety of approaches and some useful suggestions.

1. *Ten-year-old mixed group from London, who take turns to choose*

1990	Kazuo Ishiguro	*A Pale View of Hills*
	Toni Morrison	*Beloved*
	D. H. Lawrence	*The Rainbow*
	Somerset Maugham	*The Razor's Edge*
	Chinua Achebe	*Things Fall Apart*
	Nicholson Baker	*The Mezzanine*
	Christopher Hope	*My Chocolate Redeemer*
	Margaret Atwood	*Cat's Eye*
	Hilary Mantel	*Fludd*
	Richard Ford	*The Sports Writer*
1991	Julian Barnes	*A History of the World in $10\frac{1}{2}$ Chapters*
	Ian McEwan	*The Child in Time*
	A. S. Byatt	*Possession*
	Brian Moore	*Lies of Silence*
	Elizabeth Smart	*By Grand Central Station I Sat Down and Wept*

	E. M. Forster	*Where Angels Fear to Tread*
	Jane Austen	*Mansfield Park*
	Isaac Bashevis Singer	*Shosha*
	Nadine Gordimer	*Burger's Daughter*
1992	Don Delillo	*White Noise*
	Naguib Mahfouz	*The Search*
	Jennifer Johnston	*The Railway Station Man*
	V.S. Naipaul	*The Enigma of Arrival*
	E. M. Forster	*Howards End*
	George Eliot	*Middlemarch*
	Jane Gardam	*The Queen of the Tambourine*
1993	Iris Murdoch	*The Message to the Planet*
	Iris Murdoch	*A Fairly Honourable Defeat*
	Jilly Cooper	*Rivals*
	Margaret Craven	*I Heard the Owl Call My Name*
	Jane Smiley	*A Thousand Acres*
	Fyodor Dostoevsky	*Crime and Punishment*
	Flannery O'Connor	*A Good Man is Hard to Find*
	Esther Freud	*Hideous Kinky*
1994	Mikhail Bulgakov	*The Master and Margarita*
	Pat Barker	*Regeneration*
	Edith Wharton	*The Age of Innocence*
	A. S. Byatt	*The Matisse Papers*
	Joan Brady	*Theory of War*
	Virginia Woolf	*Orlando*
	Charles Dickens	*Hard Times*
	Bobbie Ann Mason	*In Country*
	Elizabeth Gaskell	*North and South*
1995	Elspeth Barker	*O Caledonia*
	E. Annie Proulx	*The Shipping News*
	Peter Hoeg	*Miss Smilla's Feeling for Snow*

	Joseph Conrad	*Heart of Darkness*
	Margaret Atwood	*The Robber Bride*
	Gita Mehta	*A River Sutra*
	George Eliot	*Daniel Deronda*
	John Banville	*The Book of Evidence*
	Alan Hollinghurst	*The Swimming Pool Library*
1996	V. S. Naipaul	*A House for Mr Biswas*
	Jeanette Winterson	*Oranges Are Not the Only Fruit*
	Kenzaburo Oe	*A Personal Matter*
	Kate Atkinson	*Behind the Scenes at the Museum*
	Willa Cather	*The Professor's House*
	Henry James	*Washington Square*
	David Guterson	*Snow Falling on Cedars*
	James Joyce	*A Portrait of the Artist as a Young Man*
1997	David Lodge	*Therapy*
	Sebastian Faulks	*Birdsong*
	George Mackay Brown	*Beside the Ocean of Time*
	Michael Ondaatje	*The English Patient*
	Graham Swift	*Last Orders*
	Rohinton Mistry	*A Fine Balance*
	Shena Mackay	*The Orchard on Fire*
	Heinrich Böll	*The Lost Honour of Katharina Blum*
1998	Graham Greene	*The End of the Affair*
	Beryl Bainbridge	*Every Man for Himself*
	William Maxwell	*So Long, See You Tomorrow*
	André Brink	*An Instant in the Wind*
	Rose Tremain	*The Way I Found Her*
	A. L. Kennedy	*So I Am Glad*
	Ted Hughes	*Birthday Letters*
	Cormac McCarthy	*All the Pretty Horses*

2. Five-year-old group who take turns to go to the central library store and pick novels that have at least eight copies available. They occasionally buy paperbacks after mutual discussion and then exchange them with two other reading groups. They also borrow from the local high school.

1994	Susan Hill	*Air and Angels*
	Iris Murdoch	*A Fairly Honourable Defeat*
	E. M. Forster	*A Passage to India*
	Barbara Comyns	*The Juniper Tree*
	Molly Keane	*Loving and Giving*
	Doris Lessing	*The Habit of Loving*
	Leo Tolstoy	*Anna Karenina*
	Polly Devlin	*Dora*
	Stella Gibbons	*Cold Comfort Farm*
	Anita Brookner	*Hotel du Lac*
	Wendy Perriam	*Devils, for a Change*
1995	Edith Wharton	*The Age of Innocence*
	Fay Weldon	*The Heart of the Country*
	A. S. Byatt	*Possession*
	Rose Tremain	*Sacred Country*
	Angela Carter	*Wise Children*
	Alan Sillitoe	*The Loneliness of the Long Distance Runner*
	Ernest Hemingway	*A Farewell to Arms*
	Carol Clewlow	*Keeping the Faith*
	Julia O'Faolain	*The Obedient Wife*
	Jane Austen	*Sense and Sensibility*
	Evelyn Waugh	*Scoop*
1996	Ivan Turgenev	*On the Eve*
	Saul Bellow	*The Victim*

E. M. Forster — *Howards End*
Mary Wesley — *Jumping the Queue*
Gabriel García Márquez — *Love in the Time of Cholera*

Radclyffe Hall — *The Well of Loneliness*
Evelyn Waugh — *A Handful of Dust*
F. Scott Fitzgerald — *The Great Gatsby*
Hilary Mantel — *Eight Months on Ghazza Street*
Gustave Flaubert — *Three Tales*

1997
Pat Barker — *Union Street*
Graham Greene — *The Heart of the Matter*
Arnold Bennett — *Anna of the Five Towns*
William Golding — *Free Fall*
Aldous Huxley — *Antic Hay*
Penelope Lively — *The Road to Lichfield*
H. E. Bates — *Fair Stood the Wind for France*
Anita Desai — *The Village by the Sea*
Henry Green — *Living*
D. H. Lawrence — *The Rainbow*
Bruce Chatwin — *The Songlines*
L. P. Hartley — *The Go-Between*
Virginia Woolf — *To the Lighthouse*

1998
Adam Thorpe — *Ulverton*
Nadine Gordimer — *Burger's Daughter*
F. Scott Fitzgerald — *Tender is the Night*
George Eliot — *Silas Marner*
Anne Tyler — *Dinner at the Homesick Restaurant*

Graham Swift — *Out of this World*
Flora Thompson — *Lark Rise to Candleford*
John Berendt — *Midnight in the Garden of Good and Evil*

Graham Greene — *The End of the Affair*

1999	Carson McCullers	*The Heart is a Lonely Hunter*
	Anthony Trollope	*The Warden*
	Wilkie Collins	*The Moonstone*
	John Irving	*A Prayer for Owen Meany*
	Victor Hugo	*The Hunchback of Notre Dame*

3. *A seven-year-old all-male urban group; the host for the evening chooses, subject to veto by two or more members.*

1992	Wilkie Collins	*The Woman in White*
	Toni Morrison	*Beloved*
	Fyodor Dostoevsky	*Notes from Underground*
	Jane Austen	*Emma*
	Jean Rhys	*The Wide Sargasso Sea*
	Willa Cather	*Lucy Gayheart*
	Gustave Flaubert	*Madame Bovary*
	Alina Reyes	*The Butcher*

1993	Aldous Huxley	*After Many a Summer*
	Martin Amis	*London Fields*
	Jean-Paul Sartre	*Nausea*
	Ernest Hemingway	*Fiesta*
	Jay McInerney	*Brightness Falls*
	George Orwell	*Homage to Catalonia*
	Joseph Conrad	*Nostromo*
	Evelyn Waugh	*Officers and Gentlemen*
	George Eliot	*Middlemarch*
	E. M. Forster	*Howards End*

1994	John Carey	*The Intellectuals and the Masses*
	Ivan Turgenev	*Fathers and Sons*
	F. Scott Fitzgerald	*The Great Gatsby*
	Henry James	*The Aspern Papers*
	Emily Brontë	*Wuthering Heights*

Patrick Suskind   *Perfume*
Cormac McCarthy   *All the Pretty Horses*
Primo Levi   *If Not Now, When?*
Louise Erdrich   *Love Medicine*
Peter Ackroyd   *Hawksmoor*
William Golding   *Rites of Passage*

1995   Charles Dickens   *Great Expectations*
R. L. Stevenson   *Kidnapped*
T. S. Eliot   *The Waste Land*
Andy McNab   *Bravo Two Zero*
E. Annie Proulx   *The Shipping News*
Gustave Flaubert   *A Sentimental Education*
Vladimir Nabokov   *Lolita*
Thomas Hardy   *The Mayor of Casterbridge*
Shusaku Endo   *Silence*

1996   Pat Barker   *Regeneration*
Jill Paton Walsh   *Knowledge of Angels*
Carol Shields   *The Stone Diaries*
Albert Camus   *The Outsider*
Virginia Woolf   *To the Lighthouse*
Jack Kerouac   *On the Road*
Rudyard Kipling   *Kim*
Isabelle Allende   *The House of the Spirits*
Richard Ford   *Independence Day*

1997   Alan Duff   *Once Were Warriors*
J. D. Salinger   *The Catcher in the Rye*
Graham Swift   *Last Orders*
Brian Moore   *The Statement*
Sebastian Faulks   *Birdsong*
William Faulkner   *As I Lay Dying*
Fyodor Dostoevsky   *Crime and Punishment*
Patrick O'Brian   *Master and Commander*

	Victor Hugo	*Les Misérables*
1998	Jeanette Winterson	*Sexing the Cherry*
	Alexander Solzhenitsyn	*The First Circle*
	Émile Zola	*Nana*
	Patricia Duncker	*Hallucinating Foucault*
	Kazuo Ishiguro	*An Artist of the Floating World*
	Anne Michaels	*Fugitive Pieces*
	Henry James	*The Portrait of a Lady*
	Louis de Bernières	*Captain Corelli's Mandolin*
	John Banville	*The Untouchable*
1999		*The Gospels*
	Harper Lee	*To Kill a Mockingbird*
	Mikhail Sholokov	*And Quiet Flows the Don*
	Flann O'Brien	*The Third Policeman*
	Norman Mailer	*The Naked and the Dead*
	Gabriel García Márquez	*One Hundred Years of Solitude*

4. *Fifteen-year-old all-female group who read only female authors; they try to vary the genres and cover as many cultures as are written in English or translated.*

1994	Shena Mackay	*Dunedin*
	Edith Wharton	*The Age of Innocence*
	Cristina Garcia	*Dreaming in Cuban*
	Jane Austen	*Persuasion*
	Jenny Uglow	*Elizabeth Gaskell*
	Joanna Trollope	*The Choir*
	Rose Zwi	*Safe Houses*
	Colette	*Ripening Seed*
	Jill Tweedie	*Eating Children: Young Dreams and Early Nightmares*
	E. Annie Proulx	*Postcards*
	Thulani Davis	*1959: a novel*

1995	Mary McCarthy	*The Group*
	Anchee Min	*Red Azalea*
	Mary Webb	*Precious Bane*
	Hilary Mantel	*A Change of Climate*
	Maryse Condé	*Tree of Life*
	Bessie Head	*A Question of Power*
	Helen Dunmore	*Burning Bright*
	Ntozake Shange	*Liliane*
	Alice Munro	*Open Secrets*
	Ann Oakley	*Taking it like a Woman*
	Lorrie Moore	*Who Will Run the Frog Hospital?*
1996	Candia McWilliam	*Debatable Land*
	Doris Lessing	*Under my Skin*
	Jill Paton Walsh	*Knowledge of Angels*
	Janet Malcolm	*The Silent Woman: Sylvia Plath and Ted Hughes*
	Denise Neuhaus	*The Christening*
	Kate Atkinson	*Behind the Scenes at the Museum*
	Frances Sherwood	*Vindication*
	Sattareh Farman Farmaian	*Daughter of Persia*
	Meera Syal	*Anita and Me*
	Emily Brontë	*Wuthering Heights*
	Mary S. Lovell	*A Scandalous Life: Biography of Jane Digby*
1997	Muriel Spark	*Symposium*
	Sylvie Germain	*The Book of Nights*
	Iris Murdoch	*Jackson's Dilemma*
	Joan Smith	*Why Aren't They Screaming?*
	Carson McCullers	*The Heart is a Lonely Hunter*
	Kate O'Brien	*The Land of Spices*
	Susan Wicks	*Driving my Father*

	Monika Fagerholm	*Wonderful Women by the Water*
	Emma Thompson	*Sense and Sensibility* (screenplay)
	Orly Castel-Bloom	*Dolly City*
1998	Rebecca West	*The Fountain Overflows*
	Arundhati Roy	*The God of Small Things*
	Barbara Kingsolver	*Animal Dreams*
	Rumer Godden	*The River*
	Barbara Pym	*A Glass of Blessings*
	Elizabeth Latham	*Silences of the Heart*
	Anne Michaels	*Fugitive Pieces*
	Paula Sharp	*Crows over a Wheatfield*
	Elizabeth Stoddard	*The Morgesons*
	Catherine Cookson	*Our Kate*
1999	Maryse Condé	*Windward Heights*
	Kiran Desai	*Hullabaloo in the Guava* *Orchard*
	Gish Jen	*Typical American*
	Claire Tomalin	*Jane Austen*
	Pamela Jooste	*Dance with a Poor Man's* *Daughter*
	Elizabeth Bowen	*The Heat of the Day*

5. *A rural group who give their books 'good read' scores out of 10.*

Joanna Trollope	*A Spanish Lover*	7.0
Susan Hill	*The Mist in the Mirror*	4.5
E. Annie Proulx	*The Shipping News*	7.4
Elizabeth Gaskell	*Mary Barton*	7.2
Ivy Compton-Burnett	various	7.0
Dorothy L. Sayers	*The Nine Tailors*	7.5
Robert Waller	*The Bridges of Madison County*	7.5

Hilary Mantel	*Fludd*	7.0
Anne Tyler	*Saint Maybe*	7.8
Willa Cather	*My Antonía*	8.3
George Eliot	*Adam Bede*	6.2
Margaret Kennedy	*The Constant Nymph*	6.2
Thomas Hardy	*A Pair of Blue Eyes*	6.2
Jane Austen	*Emma*	7.2
Jane Gardam	*Crusoe's Daughter*	6.8
Anita Brookner	*Incidents in the Rue Laugier*	6.9
Graham Swift	*Waterland*	7.3
Toni Morrison	*Beloved*	8.7
Katie fforde	*Living Dangerously*	4.4
Jostein Gaarder	*Sophie's World*	5.5
Kate Atkinson	*Behind the Scenes at the Museum*	8.5
Louis de Bernières	*Captain Corelli's Mandolin*	8.8
Giuseppe di Lampedusa	*The Leopard*	7.7
Carol Shields	*Larry's Party*	7.6
George Eliot	*Middlemarch*	8.2

6. *Twenty-seven-year-old group who choose a theme and then find books to fit it. They also bring additional poems and stories, and do play readings.*

Food	Karen Blixen	*Babette's Feast*
	Laura Esquivel	*Like Water for Chocolate*
	Margaret Atwood	*The Edible Woman*
	Alan Ayckbourn	*Table Manners*
Castles	P. G. Wodehouse	*Blandings Castle*
	Dodie Smith	*I Capture the Castle*
	Vita Sackville-West	*Pepita*
	Thomas Love Peacock	*Nightmare Abbey*
	William Douglas Home	*The Queen's Highland Servant*

Theft	Charles Williams	*Many Dimensions*
	Wilkie Collins	*The Moonstone*
	Terence Rattigan	*The Winslow Boy*
	Poems	'The Jackdaw of Rheims', etc.
Disability	Michael Howell and Peter Ford	*The True History of the Elephant Man*
	Sebastien Japrisot	*A Very Long Engagement*
	Mark Medoff	*Children of a Lesser God*

7. *Twenty-three-year-old group, who choose over an annual dinner, and sometimes read thematically. This is one year's reading, on the theme of 'men'.*

Homer	*The Odyssey*
Shakespeare	*Antony and Cleopatra*
William Thackeray	*The History of Henry Esmond*
Gerard Manley Hopkins	poems, in particular 'The Bugler's First Communion' and 'Felix Randall'
Mark Twain	*The Adventures of Huckleberry Finn*
Cormac McCarthy	*All the Pretty Horses*
Seamus Heaney	*The Spirit Level* (also in Audio Books)
Pat Barker	*Regeneration*
Nicholas Mosley	*Hopeful Monsters*

8. *Two-and-a-half-year-old group in their thirties, who compiled a booklist divided into contemporary fiction, classics, non-fiction, etc. They choose a book from the list at each meeting, with a view to varying their selections.*

Contemporary English fiction	A. S. Byatt	*Possession*
	Catherine Chidgey	*In a Fishbone Church*
	J. M. Coetzee	*Disgrace*
	Jim Crace	*Quarantine, Being Dead*
	Peter Hedges	*An Ocean in Iowa*
	Ian McEwan	*The Child in Time*
	Shena Mackay	*The Orchard on Fire*
	Hilary Mantel	*An Experiment in Love*
	Sue Miller	*While I was Gone*
	Julie Myerson	*Me and the Fat Man*
	Vikram Seth	*An Equal Music*
	Anita Shreve	*The Pilot's Wife*
Contemporary non-fiction	Tony Hawks	*Round Ireland with a Fridge*
	Giles Milton	*Nathaniel's Nutmeg*
Twentieth-century classics	Graham Greene	*Brighton Rock*
	Harper Lee	*To Kill a Mockingbird*
	Iris Murdoch	*The Bell*
	V. S. Naipaul	*A Bend in the River*
	Virginia Woolf	*To the Lighthouse*
Nineteenth-century classics	Charlotte Brontë	*Jane Eyre*
	Joseph Conrad	*Heart of Darkness*
	George Gissing	*New Grub Street*

| Thomas Hardy | *Under the Greenwood Tree* |
| Mark Twain | *The Adventures of Tom Sawyer* |

9. *Twenty-five-year-old group which meets once a week to read aloud to each other. This is a small selection.*

H. G. Wells	*The History of Mr Polly*
E. F. Benson	*Lucia Rising*
Nigel Williams	*The Wimbledon Poisoner*
Jane Hamilton	*A Map of the World*
Helen Waddell	*Peter Abelard*
Salman Rushdie	*The Moor's Last Sigh*
William Boyd	*A Good Man in Africa*
Peter Ackroyd	*Chatterton*
Helen Fielding	*Bridget Jones's Diary*
R. H. Mottram	*The Spanish Farm*
Oliver Goldsmith	*The Vicar of Wakefield*

10.   *Oprah's Book Club Selections, 2000–1*

Isabel Allende	*Daughter of Fortune*
Elizabeth Berg	*Open House*
Andre Dubus III	*House of Sand and Fog*
Jonathan Franzen	*The Corrections*
Barbara Kingsolver	*The Poisonwood Bible*
Sue Miller	*While I was Gone*
Rohinton Mistry	*A Fine Balance*
Toni Morrison	*The Bluest Eye*
Joyce Carol Oates	*We Were the Mulvaneys*
Tawni O'Dell	*Back Roads*

Malika Oufkir   *Stolen Lives: Twenty Years in*
                         a Desert Jail
Gwyn Hyman Rubio   *Icy Sparks*
Christina Schwarz   *Drowning Ruth*
Lalita Tademy   *Cane River*

11. *BBC Radio 4 Bookclub Choices*, 1998–2001

Douglas Adams   *The Hitchhiker's Guide to*
                         the Galaxy
Isabel Allende   *The House of the Spirits*
Martin Amis   *London Fields*
Kate Atkinson   *Behind the Scenes at*
                         the British Museum
Julian Barnes   *Flaubert's Parrot*
Anthony Beevor   *Stalingrad*
Geoffrey Chaucer   *The Miller's Tale*
Wendy Cope   *Making Cocoa for Kingsley*
                         Amis
Anita Desai   *Fasting, Feasting*
Margaret Drabble   *The Witch of Exmoor*
Helen Dunmore   *Talking to the Dead*
James Ellroy   *The Black Dahlia*
Margaret Forster   *Private Papers*
Charles Frazier   *Cold Mountain*
Susan Hill   *In the Springtime of the Year*
Doris Lessing   *The Grass is Singing*
Ian McEwan   *Enduring Love*
Anne Michaels   *Fugitive Pieces*
Tony Parsons   *Man and Boy*
E. Annie Proulx   *The Shipping News*
Philip Pullman   *Northern Lights*
Ian Rankin   *Knots and Crosses*
J. K. Rowling   *Harry Potter and the Philosopher's Stone*

Carol Shields	*Larry's Party*
Joe Simpson	*Touching the Void*
Dava Sobel	*Longitude*
Graham Swift	*Waterland*
Amy Tan	*The Kitchen God's Wife*
Joanna Trollope	*Other People's Children*

12. *YOU Reading Group, Books of the Month, 1998–2001*

1998	Louis de Bernières	*Captain Corelli's Mandolin**
	Beryl Bainbridge	*Every Man for Himself**
	Margaret Forster	*Lady's Maid*
	Jane Smiley	*A Thousand Acres*
	Arthur Golden	*Memoirs of a Geisha*
	Jane Hamilton	*Map of the World*
	Margaret Atwood	*Alias Grace*
	Sue Grafton	*M is for Malice*
	Ian McEwan	*Enduring Love*
	Carol Shields	*Larry's Party*
	David Guterson	*Snow Falling on Cedars*
	Nick Hornby	*Fever Pitch*
1999	Stella Tillyard	*The Aristocrats**
	Amanda Foreman	*Georgiana Duchess of Devonshire**
	Frank McCourt	*Angela's Ashes**
	Barbara Kingsolver	*The Poisonwood Bible*
	Helen Dunmore	*Your Blue-Eyed Boy*
	Charles Frazier	*Cold Mountain*
	Jane Gardam	*The Queen of the Tambourine*
	Bernhard Schlink	*The Reader*
	Joanna Trollope	*Other People's Children*
	Maggie Gee	*The Ice People*

	Jonathan Coe	*What a Carve-Up*
	Ronan Bennett	*The Catastrophist*
2000	Joanne Harris	*Chocolat**
	Sebastian Faulks	*Charlotte Gray*
	Deborah Moggach	*Tulip Fever*
	James Fox	*The Langhorne Sisters*
	Melvyn Bragg	*The Soldier's Return**
	Rose Tremain	*The Way I Found Her*
	Isabel Allende	*Daughter of Fortune*
	Michael Frayn	*Headlong*
	Nancy Mitford	*Love in a Cold Climate*
	Judith Thurman	*Secrets of the Flesh, A Life of Colette*
	Elinor Lipman	*The Ladies' Man*
	Anita Shreve	*The Pilot's Wife*
2001	Melissa Bank	*The Girls' Guide to Hunting and Fishing*
	Joanna Trollope	*Marrying the Mistress**
	Patrick McGrath	*Asylum*
	Kazuo Ishiguro	*When We Were Orphans*
	Kate Atkinson	*Emotionally Weird*
	Anne Tyler	*Ladder of Years**
	Maggie O'Farrell	*After You'd Gone**
	Margaret Forster	*The Memory Box*
	Anne Fine	*Telling Liddy*
	Christina Schwarz	*Drowning Ruth*
	Jill Dawson	*Fred and Edie*
	Carol Shields	*Jane Austen*

* *YOU* reading group top ten titles

13. *A selection of books popular during* 2001 *with the* 500 *book clubs affiliated to the Tattered Cover bookstore in Denver, Colorado. Virginia Valentine, the book clubs co-ordinator for Tattered Cover, comments that historical novels are doing well, as are books about the Muslim world.*

Charles Baxter	*The Feast of Love*
Michelle de Krester	*The Rose Grower*
Gloria Emerson	*Loving Graham Greene*
Claire Messud	*The Last Life*
Manil Suri	*The Death of Vishnu*
Gail Tsukiyama	*The Samurai's Garden*
Geraldine Brooks	*Nine Parts of Desire*
Rosa Shand	*The Gravity of Sunlight*
Anita Diamant	*The Red Tent*
Barbara Kingsolver	*Prodigal Summer*

14. *The Ivanhoe Reading Circle from Victoria, Australia, celebrated its eightieth anniversary in* 2000; *here is its reading list from that year. A large group of forty to fifty members with ages ranging from late thirties to over* 90, *it owes its success to the vigour of its traditions, a willingness to take off in new directions (its current interest in contemporary Australian literature for instance), and the loyalty of its membership—Vere Duncan served as secretary for seventy-two years. The group's history, with a list of their reading over eighty years,* Walking with the Gods *by Stephanie Berry, is published by Spectrum Publications Pty Ltd, email spectpub@ozemail.com.au.*

Murray Bail	*Eucalyptus*
Susanne Chick	*Searching for Charmian*
Anne Chisholm	*Rumer Godden*
Michael Cunningham	*The Hours*
Louis de Bernières	*Captain Corelli's Mandolin*
Janet Gleeson	*The Arcanum*
Thomas Hardy	*Far From the Madding Crowd* (last read in 1954)
Tom Stoppard	*Arcadia*

15. *Books read by UK groups in 2001: a selection from the non-fiction titles*

Martin Amis	*Experience*
Christabel Bielenberg	*The Past is Myself*
Isabella Bird	*A Lady's Life in the Rocky Mountains*
Dirk Bogarde	*Cleared for Take-off*
Tim Clayton and Phil Craig	*Finest Hour*
Patrick Leigh Fermor	*A Time of Gifts*
Isabel Fonseca	*Bury Me Standing*
Benjamin Foster, ed.	*The Epic of Gilgamesh*
Brian Friel	*Translations*
Annie Hawes	*Extra Virgin*
Michael Holroyd	*Basil Street Blues*
Kay Redfield Jamison	*An Unquiet Mind*
Penelope Lively	*Oleander, Jacaranda*
Diane Middlebrook	*Suits Me: The Double Life of Billy Tipton*
Samuel Pepys	*The Diary of Samuel Pepys*
Gervase Phinn	*The Other Side of the Dale*
Sylvia Plath	*Letters Home*
Jonathan Raban	*Passage to Juneau*

Silvia Rodgers	*Red Saint, Pink Daughter*
Betty Schimmel	*To See You Again*
Chris Stewart	*Driving Over Lemons*

16. Books read by UK groups in 2001: a selection from the books read in translation

Albert Camus	*The Plague*
Louis-Ferdinand Celine	*Journey to the end of the Night*
Anton Chekhov	*Lady with Lapdog and Other Stories*
Marie Darrieussecq	*My Phantom Husband*
Gunther Grass	*The Tin Drum*
Michel Houellebecq	*Atomised*
Andrey Kurkov	*Death and the Penguin*
Par Lagerkvist	*Barabbas*
Mikhail Lermontov	*A Hero of Our Time*
Niccolo Machiavelli	*The Prince*
Haruki Murakami	*The Wind-Up Bird Chronicle*
Dorit Peleg	*Miss Fanny's Voice*
Arturo Perez-Reverte	*The Fencing Master*
Erich Maria Remarque	*All Quiet on the Western Front*
Yasmina Reza	*Hammerklavier*
W. G. Sebald	*The Rings of Saturn*
Beat Sterchi	*The Cow*
Wladyslaw Szpilman	*The Pianist*

17. Books read by UK groups in 2001: collections of short stories

| Richard Ford | *A Multitude of Sins* |
| Susan Hill, ed. | *The Penguin Book of Contemporary Women's Short Stories* |

M. R. James	*Ghost Stories*
James Joyce	*Dubliners*
Jhumpa Lahiri	*Interpreter of Maladies*
Katherine Mansfield	*'The Garden Party' and Other Stories*
W. Somerset Maugham	*The Collected Stories*, Vols 1 and 2
Saki (H. H. Munro)	*The Best of Saki*
Elaine Showalter, ed.	*Scribbling Women* (short stories by American women writers)
William Trevor	*The Collected Stories*
H. G. Wells	*The Time Machine*

18. *Books read by UK groups in 2001, titles by children's authors*

David Almond	*Heaven Eyes*
Hans Christian Andersen	*'The Snow Queen' and Other Fairy Tales and Legends*
Lewis Carroll	*Alice in Wonderland, Alice through the Looking Glass*
Kenneth Grahame	*The Wind in the Willows*
Ted Hughes	*The Iron Man*
C. S. Lewis	*The Lion, the Witch and the Wardrobe*
Joan Lingard	*Dreams of Love and Modest Glory*
L. M. Montgomery	*Anne of Green Gables*
William Nicholson	*The Wind Singer*
J. K. Rowling	The Harry Potter books
Philip Pullman	*His Dark Materials* trilogy
J. R. R. Tolkein	*The Hobbit*

19. *Books read by UK groups in 2001: two groups choose by theme, the first is a library-based group.*

A Taste of the East:

Fiction   Amy Tan *The Bonesetter's Daughter*
Kathryn Harrison *The Binding Chair*
Arthur Golden *Memoirs of a Geisha*
Alex Garland *The Beach*
J. G. Ballard *Empire of the Sun*
Oswald Wynd *The Ginger Tree*
Ann Bridge *Peking Picnic*
James Clavell *Shogun*
Kazuo Ishiguro *An Artist of the Floating World*
Emily Prager 'A Visit from the Footbinder'
   (short story)

Non-fiction   William Dalrymple *In Xanadu*
Marco Polo et al. *The Travels of Marco Polo*
Colin Mason *A Short History of Asia*
Nick Middleton *The Last Disco in Outer Mongolia*
Jung Chang *Wild Swans*
Adeline Yen Mah *Falling Leaves*, *Falling Leaves Return to their Roots*
Sue Arnold *A Burmese Legacy*
Christopher West *Journey to the Middle Kingdom*
Gavin Young *Slow Boats to China*
Han Suyin *My House has Two Doors*

A group which meets in term-time, and picks a theme a term:

Conflicts: Olivia Manning *The Great Fortune*
Charles Dickens *A Tale of Two Cities*
Charles Frazier *Cold Mountain*

Christopher Fry *The Dark is Light Enough*, (play-reading)
Short stories and extracts chosen by group members

Work: David Lodge *Nice Work*
Extracts from e.g. Cellini's *Memoirs*, Kilvert's *Diary*
Willa Cather *O Pioneers!*
Robert Bolt *Flowering Cherry*, (play-reading)

Victorian Lives: Anthony Trollope *An Autobiography*
Claire Tomalin *Invisible Woman*
Lynne Reid Banks *Dark Quartet*
Victorian letters chosen by group members

20. *A UK group who give their books marks out of ten. This is their reading for* 2001; *they point out that* White Teeth *and* Death in Holy Orders *had the most extreme marking.*

Author	Title	Average Mark	Range of Mark
Bruce Chatwin	*On the Black Hill*	7	6–8
Rose Tremain	*Music and Silence*	7	6–8
Rose Macaulay	*The Towers of Trebizond*	5.5	4–8
D. H. Lawrence	*Sons and Lovers*	6	5–7
Helen Dunmore	*Burning Bright*	7	7–8
Zadie Smith	*White Teeth*	6	2–8
Margaret Atwood	*The Handmaid's Tale*	6	3–8

Author	Title	Average Mark	Range of Mark
Tracy Chevalier	*Girl with a Pearl Earring*	7	6–8
M. E. Braddon	*Lady Audley's Secret*	6.5	5–8
Amy Tan	*The Hundred Secret Senses*	7.5	7–9
George Orwell	*The Road to Wigan Pier*	6	4–9
Helen Dunmore	*The Siege*	7	6–8
P. D. James	*Death in Holy Orders*	7	3–9

Further Reading

Altick, Richard D., *The English Common Reader* (Chicago and London: University of Chicago Press, 1957).

Cavallo, Guglielmo, and Chartier, Roger (eds.), *A History of Reading in the West*, trans. Lydia G. Cochrane (Cambridge: Polity Press, 1999).

Darnton, Robert, *The Kiss of Lamourette* (London: Faber and Faber, 1990).

Davidson, Cathy N. (ed.), *Reading in America* (Baltimore and London: Johns Hopkins University Press, 1989).

Finkelstein, David and McCleery, Alistair (eds.), *The Book History Reader* (London and New York: Routledge, 2002).

Flint, Kate, *The Woman Reader, 1837–1914* (Oxford: Clarendon Press, 1993).

Manguel, Alberto, *A History of Reading* (London: HarperCollins, 1996).

Pearson, Jacqueline, *Women's Reading in Britain 1750–1835: A Dangerous Recreation* (Cambridge: Cambridge University Press, 1999).

Radway, Janice, *A Feeling for Books: The Book-of-the-Month Club, Literary Taste, and Middle-Class Desire* (Chapel Hill and London: University of North Carolina Press, 1997).

Raven, James, Small, Helen, and Taylor, Naomi (eds.), *The Practice and Representation of Reading in England* (Cambridge: Cambridge University Press, 1996).

Rose, Jonathan, *The Intellectual Life of the British Working Classes* (New Haven: Yale University Press, 2001).

Thebridge, Stella, et al, *Partnership in Promotion: Publishers, Booksellers and Libraries Working Together to Promote Reading* (Birmingham: Centre for Information Research, 2001).

Todd, Richard, *Consuming Fictions: The Booker Prize and Fiction in Britain Today* (London: Bloomsbury, 1996).

Reading Group Survey

About the group

1 How long has your group been going?

2 How did it start? (one person, a group of friends, did you all know each other beforehand?)

3 What made you want to join?

4 Does membership remain constant? Is there a waiting list?

5 How often do you meet, and how many usually attend?

6 Where do you meet (each other's homes?), and for how long?

7 Do you serve food and/or drink? Do you make time for social chat before or after the group?

8 Is the group all male/all female/mixed?

9 What is the average age of the group (roughly)?

10 Are you in a rural, urban or suburban area?

11 Have some of you been in higher education? Please give a rough percentage.

12 Are you in paid work, and if so, full-time or part-time? Again, please give rough percentages.

What you read

13 Please tick the categories you have read in your group:
    Fiction, contemporary
    Fiction, 20th-century

Fiction, pre-20th-century
Non-fiction, biography, memoirs
Poetry
Other

14 Which categories have you read most of?

15 Do you read more books by men or by women, or would you say that the sex of the author is not important to you?

16 How do you choose what to read?

17 Is the price of the book important when you are choosing? Do you mainly borrow or buy?

18 How do you structure your discussions? Do you have a leader; how is s/he chosen; do you have discussion notes or use readers' guides?

19 Does your discussion tend to stick to the text, or range more widely? If so, what sort of issues come up?

20 Please list ten books you've recently read in the group, or as many as you can.

21 Could you name one book which went well and explain why?

22 Could you name one book which went badly and explain why?

23 Do most group members manage to finish the book?

24 What do you most enjoy about your reading group?

25 Has the group changed at all since its beginnings? If so, in what ways?

We hope to do some follow-up work with some of the groups. If your group might be prepared for one of us to sit in on a meeting, please indicate below, with a contact name and address.